B IT'S NO JOKE
EING
DEAF

The autobiography of a man
of many skills, but born deaf

Michael Jack

CORTNEY PUBLICATIONS ASHWELL

DEDICATION

To dearest Audrey
with loving gratitude for
53 years' companionship.

ISBN 0 904378 43 8

Published by
Cortney Publications,
57 Ashwell Street, Ashwell,
Baldock, Herts SG7 5QT

Cover design by Colin Baker (Whaddon)
Page preparation by Word Design Technology (Clifton)
Reproduction film by Monographics (Dunstable)
Printing and Binding by
Woolnough Bookbinding Ltd (Irthlingborough)

Contents

Introduction

My first book was inspired by the series of articles which appeared over a period of twenty years in the RNID journals., Silent World and Hearing. I thought all the material deserved a new lease of life in book form and my first editor, Roy Cole, did the initial work of collating the articles into a semblance of order.

Its publication in 1981 resulted in many letters of appreciation especially from deaf people who wrote to tell me that they had no idea that someone else could suffer in similar ways and how encouraged they were to read of my experiences. Other people asked for a further book touching on topics barely mentioned earlier – dowsing, for example.

So this book is the result. Nearly three years of hard work have been involved, sandwiched between mowing lawns, cutting churchyards and gardening. Now I have cold feet. No one will want to buy and read it! But writing is a relaxation for me and has been ever since my first article appeared in Musical Opinion in 1959, encouraged by the noted writer on organs, Noel Bonavia-Hunt. This was about Organists' Twitching Fingers, mentioned in the text and the forerunner of twenty years of articles on organists and choirs, including my poor great uncle Alexander Holt, and local history articles in Kent Life and By-Gone Kent.

If it's no joke being deaf, as the book title has it, life has brought much enjoyment and laughter has never been far away. Its tribulations have often driven me to follow pursuits and develop interests which have given pleasures that otherwise might have been missed.

All these have been reflected in my writings which I hope will enable you, the reader to share in my "ups and downs", enjoy the humour and give you a "good read".

Michael Jack

THE BBC's *SEE HEAR!* TEAM VISITS THE AUTHOR
(September 1983)

Above: *The Team photographed in the Author's garden.*

Below: *The Team visiting Newington churchyard. It later visited a water company field in Hythe, where I successfully demonstrated dowsing.*

Author's Note: My neighbour's daughter, Audrey Williams kindly made me a video of the programme on *See Hear!* I subsequently recorded over it. Maggie Woolley, advised me to ask *See Hear!* for a replacement copy: very kindly I was sent one free of charge.

CHAPTER ONE

Early Years

I have a very early memory of a doctor vaccinating me by sticking something like a potato crisp on my arm which he produced out of an old cigar box. Another memory of my friend Ann and I sitting on chamber pots on a purple carpet in the nursery, howling our heads off as soap was shoved up our bottoms to produce a 'good movement'. In similar vein years later my nurse tried to make me eat up my food by pushing it down my throat with her finger . . . something that aroused yells and tears of rage and lasting resentment.

My father had returned from the first War and rented a house in Chepstow Villas, Bayswater. Baby Michael arrived at the end of February 1920 and was installed at the top of the house with his Nanny, a climb of seventy-two stairs. In the mornings I was wheeled in my pram to the park to meet other children and their nannies in Kensington Gardens, My mother maintained I was the smartest baby in the Gardens but I fear this may have been maternal wishful thinking.

When I was two and a half my father took us for a holiday in Ostend and he organised a trip to the western front trenches. He had served as a captain in the RAMC Field Ambulance after qualifying as a doctor at the Middlesex Hospital and he gained a Military Cross at Escarmain (near Cambrai) nine days before the war ended. No doubt he wished to show my mother the conditions under which he had been fighting. I guess the trenches must have been pretty well as the armies had left them three years earlier and I have a very clear memory of walking along a trench and diving down into a dugout. It left a lasting memory of horrible fear, awful desolation and despair. It was an unexplained enigma all my life and I never understood why it had made such an impression on my infant mind. Sixty-five years later I returned to the Ypres and Somme battlefields and realised that my childhood memories were psychic ones. The trenches were saturated with the thoughts of the soldiers who had lived, suffered and died in those trenches.

Nanny Marshall arrived soon after my birth and she took complete charge of my welfare; she stayed until I was five, then she emigrated to Queensland Australia to marry an unknown widower with two children. I kept in touch with her until she died in her nineties. She was replaced, first by a nurse – the one who tried force feeding me – and then by three successive governesses. Only the middle lady remains in mind because she was French and possessed red hair and a temper to match. Battles with Mam'selle were non-stop. She took me for a walk once and I found a large heavy tree branch maybe ten feet long which I decided to take home with us. It proved heavy to drag behind me along the road so I delegated this duty to Mam'selle, who obediently began pulling it behind her but when I was not looking she dropped it. I soon cottoned on to her perfidy, ran back, picked up the branch and hit her over the head with it. This led to the usual outburst of temper, terminating as it always did, with screams of rage and: "You 'orrible nasty hateful beastly little boy, MIGULL!". My parents must have realised we were not suited to each other and Mam'selle disappeared soon afterwards, perhaps before one of us put the other into hospital.

In the early nineteen-twenties my father drove a two-seater Singer motor with a dickey. We travelled all over the country in it, to Devon and Cornwall and Thetford in Norfolk. My parents sat in front (with the hood up in bad weather), Nanny or Ann and I in the dickey, exposed to all that the elements could throw at us. I daresay modern drivers would regard us with pitying horror but it never did us any harm and maybe laid the foundation for my excellent health over the years coupled with a dislike for over-heated homes and shops and further strengthened by the rigours of public school boarding.

I remember only two incidents – one of my father driving the Singer on to the sands at Polzeith when the tide was out and as the sea returned, the firm sand turned to quicksands and the car began to sink. All the surf riders rallied round, dug their surf boards under the wheels and dragged the little vehicle back to firm ground.

The other incident at Polzeith concerned Ann. She was the daughter of my mother's oldest friend, my Godmother Grace Eaton – whose photograph, incidentally, was blazoned on hoardings all over the country advertising Craven A cigarettes. Ann and I had been sitting on the beach when a huge wave roared up from nowhere, engulfed me and would have carried me away had not Ann grabbed hold of my hair and thereby saved me from drowning. She was four and I was two and a half. Seventy years later we were having an argument and Ann unkindly wondered if saving my life had been a Good Idea. I also owed her gratitude for the time when I had taken my mother's new green felt hat and thrown it into a bath of waste engine oil. I don't know why – doubtless at the time it seemed the only thing to do. My mother was furious and said I was to have no sweets for a week. "Very well then Aunty V," piped up Ann. "Then I won't have any sweets either!".

In 1924 we moved to Gerrards Cross, Buckinghamshire. In 1927 I started at the preparatory school ten minutes' walk up the road – Thorpe House. Soon afterward my parents spent a long holiday in Malta with my mother's younger brother, then Captain Holt in the regular army and I was made a boarder while they were away. I had no brothers or sisters because my arrival had been such a business that my mother vowed never to experience anything like that again. She was convinced that I would become a spoilt only child if stern measures were not taken so the boarding became permanent although my home was so near. In my place at home my parents took in my best friend Teddy Rose, who lived opposite us in Kingsway until his father deserted his wife and two small boys. He attended Thorpe House as a day boy and the knowledge that he was living at home in my place did nothing for my confidence and make me feel wanted. Then the move to Merchant Taylors School in 1933 destroyed what little I had left. From being a large fish in a small pool – head boy and in football and cricket teams – I became a totally insignificant fish in a very large pool – and a deaf fish at that.

My father became a keen golfer, joining Gerrards Cross Golf Club. He spent most weekends at the club, eventually becoming Club Captain – a position which my mother was heard to remark bitterly kept him at the club all the time, instead of most of it. My mother's family, Holt, had been lawyers for generations back to the 18th century and she was a stickler for punctuality. She insisted that Saturday and Sunday luncheons were served at one o'clock and she had a cook and a housemaid to ensure this took place. My mother and I took our places and were served with our helpings and my father never came in before one-thirty. No amount of nagging made the least difference and after lunch he returned to the club for the rest of the day. I suppose the golf round – and the nineteenth hole – took a certain time and lunch at one-thirty would have been more sensible. But that was the way it went ...

If the weather was too bad for golf my father often went to Uxbridge to listen to records and try sheet music on a piano in Willis' Music Emporium. He played the piano very well although entirely self taught. I still have all his music, which comes out of its case full of snuff; I sneeze so fast that I cannot see to read the music. He took up snuff in his later years after giving up smoking.

His other great hobby in the nineteen twenties was wireless and many weekends were spent in his workshop building complicated radio sets and amplifiers from plans printed in Wireless World. He was never content to build simple equipment but worked on progressively larger efforts. As completed, they were installed in the sitting room in a cupboard by the fireplace and it soon expanded into another cupboard on the other side. This satisfied him for a time but further advances were made in wireless technology – the screen grid valve, for example, so all his equipment disappeared from the sitting room back into the

My father and mother.

My father's first car.

Above: *The author with his mother and* (right) *with his Nanny* (on left side) *(1920's).*

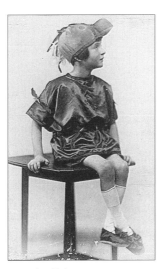

Michael with "Old Bill" the gardener at Bailsend (1925).

1st Prize as a parrot.

Michael and his friend Teddy Rose, see p.3, Thorpe House (1930).

workshop. Later on even larger and more complicated sets made their appearance and began to be installed in the sitting room cupboards. A crisis arose – there was no more room to fit in all the new units and my mother put her foot down. She had always grumbled furiously at the encroachment on her preserves – to wit, her sitting room – and now said there must be positively No More Radio Nonsense . . . It was becoming Beyond a Joke and All Reason!

So what was my poor father to do? All this splendid new equipment sitting in his workshop and nowhere to install it. He was next observed constantly in my day nursery, the other side of the sitting room, looking into my toy cupboard and making calculations in a little notebook. He then suggested that I rented him the ground shelf in my cupboard – to which I agreed. The cupboard was stuffed to bursting point with all the toys given to an only child but I had little choice but to agree. Holes were bored through the wall and the floor was completely covered with his amplifiers. Of course, my father did not intend me to suffer from losing my cupboard space and he offered me a rent of a shilling a year (5p) which my mother said was the meanest thing she had ever heard of!

I was sold the idea of building my own modest little set with valves, my cat's whisker crystal sets were never successful. So I acquired a collection of resistances, coils, condensers, volume control, reaction control, two valves – detector and amplifier . There was a low tension battery, a high tension battery of 120 volts and a grid bias battery of 9 volts. Exactly why the grid was biased or what it did when it was not biased, I never found out. I assembled the set on a plywood base, working from a plan supplied by my father and checked by him when finished. It was switched on and nothing happened. Even twiddling the reaction knob produced only silence instead of the expected ear-splitting howls. I believe the battery was flat but by then the set had vanished into my father's workshop.

We moved to Rickmansworth in 1934 and by then radiograms were in common use and my father no longer made his own sets; he bought a succession of radiograms instead. In his quest for even better quality he was always changing the sets and it was never unusual for me to come home from school and find a new radiogram. A grand piano figures in all my memories back to 1924 and they changed quite often too. We played a Bluthner for a long time but Father always wanted a Steinway and eventually one arrived . . . Only it turned out to be a Steinweg, not the same thing at all although it was a fine piano. It was only when just writing this that I realised Steinweg could be translated as Steinway!

During the war he was given a lovely sweet-toned Broadwood upright which went into his outside den and he spent many hours composing music and songs. In his eighties, when I possessed a tape recorder, my father had me record him playing all his favourite pieces, announcing each one before he played it, ending up with: "Thank you,

Mike". A lovely memorial of those happy days. He had to give up golf because of the petrol shortage.

To hark back to his radio interests again. In his constant search for really fine reproduction my father arrived at the ultimate solution – The Panatrope. This was a huge amplifier of advanced design with a loudspeaker unit that must have weighed fourteen pounds and it employed a circuit of such astoundingly high voltage as to strike dead anyone foolish enough to put his hand inside the cabinet when it was switched on. There was no room in the sitting room for this new acquisition and General Headquarters (as represented by my mother) would never have allowed it. So it was placed in the coal cellar, conveniently underneath the sitting room and large holes were bored through the floor boards to allow the sound to float upwards.

This met with grudging acceptance by my mother, still carrying on her reign of terror against overmuch intrusion in the sitting room but by an extraordinary chance the Great Panatrope Project came to naught! It was sitting in the cellar wired up and awaiting its trial run the next weekend when the coal men arrived and shot down a ton of coke through the cellar shute, completely burying the Panatrope. Exactly how much was due to my mother's artful scheming I do not know but my father lost heart, abandoned the idea and bought a really splendid Murphy console, by far the best producer of musical sound we had ever owned.

An echo of my father's interests was passed on to his grandsons Nicholas and Nigel who have always owned the latest equipment in London and Holland. I especially remember Nigel experimenting with my Magnavox radiogram when he somehow managed to introduce a full mains voltage into the loudspeaker circuit, thereby blowing all the transistors in one terrific explosion. Although repaired at huge expense – my expense – it was never the same instrument again.

After our move to Rickmansworth my mother took up riding and patronised the stables at Chorleywood several times weekly. I had received lessons from the local postman in Gerrards Cross from the age of six and went out with my mother, more from a sense of duty than from any love of horses.

I was sent out hunting with the Old Berkeley when I was seventeen with no particular wish to take part and by great good fortune disgraced myself. I was passing through a wood, presumably in pursuit of a fox – although I never clapped eyes on anything even remotely resembling a fox from start to finish. I was riding through this wood when a branch inserted itself between the saddle and my seat; the horse ambled on and I was given the old heave-ho. The horse obligingly waited for me to remount and make speedy tracks back to the stables, just the excuse I needed to abandon the hunt. My mother was furious, said I had let the side down and if I entertained any further ideas about hunting (which I did not), I could forget about them.

Because of our riding connection with Chorleywood we sometimes attended the local church on the common. The Vicar was a fiery preacher who at one point would sink his voice to a whisper and next lean over his pulpit and blare out some denunciation. He had a trick of addressing himself to members of the congregation: "Mrs Smith, your husband is out playing golf. Go and fetch him, we will wait for you". My mother was once a victim although not mentioned by name. "This morning I saw three women riding on the common before breakfast," he said quietly. He almost threw himself out of the pulpit as he yelled at the top of his voice: "THEY ARE GOING STRAIGHT TO HELL!!". My mother was in the congregation and took it as a huge joke.

She possessed a fine sense of humour which stood her in good stead when we were having tea in Marshall and Snelgrove. She overheard a lady at the next table say to her companion: "Don't you think that the lady in purple is a fine looking woman?" My mother looked about her and as no one else was wearing purple the speaker must be referring to her and mentally glowed at the compliment, only to be deflated instantly by the reply: "Well, yes my dear – if you admire the haggard type . . ."

Before the dreaded moments when I was due back at Merchant Taylors my mother used to take me out somewhere and once she took me to the Windmill Theatre. You might suppose that everyone knew about The Windmill and its nude tableaux but not my mother! The curtain rose and there was a fine display of female charms which left almost nothing to the imagination. My mother gave a gasp of sheer horror and half rose from her seat. "We must leave at once," she began, fearful of her dear only son's morals being ruined for life but fortunately my wiser counsels prevailed. No doubt I pointed out that the spectacle would take my mind off my impending doom . . .

The Windmill episode reminds me of something witnessed by my brother-in-law in a north country theatre during his RAF moves around the country in the last war. On the billing was Gloria and her Seven Glorious Nudes and in due course the curtain went up and there was Gloria and her friends displaying their charms.

There was complete silence . . . Until a child's clear treble penetrated all parts of the theatre. "Mummy – look at those ladies' titties!". Which, as they say, brought the house down.

During my earlier years and especially when I was a medical student at the Middlesex Hospital, my father's practice was the London headquarters for all our family. After his day's work was done my father frequently operated in nursing homes and we waited for him to return to Queen Anne Street before going to theatres or dinner parties. There is a mouth condition where wisdom teeth come down from the roof of the mouth and my father was a specialist surgeon in their removal; the operation could take up to two hours. He was Consultant Dental Surgeon to St Marks Hospital, giving his services freely – as did other consultants before the National Health Service started. He was then forced to accept a fee, for which he neither asked nor needed.

Two peculiar events took place about this time. My father borrowed my mother's Ford 10, returned later in the day and left it outside the back door in the stable yard. When he came out again the car had been reduced to a heap of ashes. We decided he must have dropped a lighted cigarette down between the seats and it had smouldered until the upholstery caught fire. My mother maintained she had swept up the ashes and deposited them in the dustbin but then, she never allowed the strict truth to spoil a good story . . .

On the other occasion plumbers were doing some work in our Georgian loo and went off for lunch. My mother happened to pay a visit soon afterwards and discovered the men had not only left their blowlamp roaring away but the flame was directed against the wood work which was already starting to char. She remonstrated severely with the men when they returned from lunch but they were quite unperturbed. "Oh yes Mum", one of them said. "That does happen occasionally . . ."

Another story about my father concerns the time he went into Marmite in a big way, spreading it on all his bread. A little later he noticed that his waterworks were producing a fizzy liquid and betook himself off to his doctor. The latter asked for details of his diet and when he learnt about the Marmite intake he told my father that his problem was caused by the yeast in the Marmite: his internal system had set up a kind of brewery and was producing something that could be akin to an alcoholic drink!

My friend Ann, whose mother (my godmother) was well known in advertisements for Craven A and myself at Gerrards Cross (1926).

9

CHAPTER TWO

Merchant Taylors School

In September 1933 I moved from prep. school to my public school. There were five of us boys sharing a taxi from Gerrards Cross station; it was a Daimler which had the old style motor which belched forth vast clouds of blue smoke. After the move to Rickmansworth I was able to carry on catching the taxi since it actually passed by our door. Then came the terrible day in January 1935 when I started as a reluctant boarder in The Manor of the Rose – the boarding house which held fifty poor wretched prisoners under the benign housemastership of the Reverend D. Davies. Because I was fifteen during the term I was compelled to join the Officers' Training Corps about which I have already written and my splendid and successful efforts at gaining my release. Maybe I treated it light-heartedly but that period was an abjectly unhappy one – homesickness, living a twenty-minute cycle ride from home, the difficulties with the OTC drilling compounded by my deafness; apparently the only boy in the school with a hearing problem – misunderstood by the school in general and not even considered to be a problem.

No one to turn to for help, abandoned by my parents to my fate. The only thing to do was to Run Away and I did this one Saturday afternoon in the spring, cycling into Rickmansworth and buying a pound of chocolate wholemeal biscuits in Woolworths – which cost me a shilling and fourpence, say 7p. I then made my way up to Heronsgate village on the hill above my home and sat in a field, ruminating on my life. It stretched into an infinite future of unhappiness, deserted by my parents, considered a fool by everybody at school, the end of term at least five centuries away by my jaundiced reckoning. In a sea of misery I decided there was only one thing to do and that was to End It All.

But how was I to do it with only my cycle clips and the bag of half-eaten biscuits? Not the sort of tools needed to take one's life . . . I saw the barbed wire fence and decided to Open A Vein (thinking in capitals again). I dragged my arm up and down the barbs and it proved unexpectedly painful; I acquire a fine set of scratches but was no nearer to encouraging my blood to pour out in foaming torrents.

Had I either the guts of a woodlouse or the courage of a lion I would have tried much harder or pedalled away to London and found myself a job. Possessing neither quality I cycled down the hill and gave myself up. (That looks better in capitals again – Gave Myself Up). Of course my father immediately telephoned The Manor, warning Mr. Davies to expect a runaway and drove me straight back to prison. 'DD' looked at me sadly and said: "Why didn't you trust me, Michael?" Which, after all these years, still strikes me as the silliest question I've ever been asked. What deeply homesick desperately unhappy schoolboy of fifteen, with a hearing problem (with which no one had the slightest sympathy) would trust a schoolmaster?

DD's solution was to enrol me in his Confirmation class, presumably hoping that dealing with the Almighty and learning, among other things, the Ten Commandments, would effectively reconcile me to my lot. "Put your trust in the Lord," he said but I found it all a hollow sham. As far as I could see, the Lord was totally uninterested in me and my problems – if indeed He existed at all. However, He works in strange ways. By attending chapel and joining the Manor choir I acquired a life-long interest in church music.

As a piano teacher I had Kendall Taylor who later achieved some fame as a recitalist. He was a failure as far as I was concerned and I found little to interest me in the music he set and I did little practising – all right, I was lazy! Finally my father refused to stump up another penny towards my musical education – and small blame to him. But I carried on playing, having been given permission to use the music rooms when ever I wished. I had started learning the piano from the age of seven in Gerrards Cross.

Among the more memorable masters at MTS was Charles Lummis, my form master for a year. He was useless dealing with anyone possessing a disability and he could be quite cruel – in a hearty public school way – without actually meaning to be. About the time I entered his class my father had bought me a Fortiphone hearing aid, which did offer some help in following classes although it had no volume control. I forgot it one morning and Lummis called out: "Hello Jack, where's your telephone?" immediately adding: "Oh, I was told by the headmaster not to mention it". This killed stone dead any notion of persevering with the Fortiphone and caused me lasting resentment.

Otherwise I did quite well under his tuition. He took the view that volunteering for anything was nonsense. While he told our class he hoped all the boys would volunteer to run in the school sports – where of course he hoped his form would beat everybody else – any boy who failed to volunteer would find himself being 'bumped' by the rest of the class. During a lesson in French I had to translate: The mountains of

Scotland are not so high as the Alps. He pounced on me at once: "The mountains of ScoOtland, boy, not ScUtland". So I started again: "The mountains of Scootland . . ." "Hear that?", Lummis yelled at the class. "Hear that? Confounded cheek! You can have a caning for that".

Our classrooms had large windows which opened upwards by means of a long screw device turned with a handle. Lummis, in his usual fashion, sometimes had members of the class to try and break the record for opening the windows. With his cane half out of the desk he paused. "Tell you what," he said, "If you can lower the window opening record I'll let you off the caning". Of course I agreed. He got out his stop watch and called: "On your mark . . . OFF!" I tore up to the first window and started unwinding furiously. The key flew off its squared nut and hit me above the eyebrow, causing a copious flow of blood. "Oh heck," said Lummis regretfully and sent me off to the scouts' hall to be patched up and on my return we agreed to call it quits. I was pleased as in spite of all the blood, it had not hurt at all but of course I put on a terrific act.

He took my class for School Certificate history and he had developed a system of cramming certain aspects of the syllabus based on questions set over past years. He might suggest that there had been no questions on James I for several years: it would be worth while paying special attention to the period 1603 to 1625. Or the Civil War could be discounted as this had appeared three times in five years.

I followed his advice, gained a credit in history – above one of my essays – on English Seamen in the 16th Century – he had written GOOD STUFF!! But I also gained credits in English, Mathematics, Chemistry, Physics, Biology and a Pass in French which meant I was excused sitting the Matriculation examination for London University, of which the Middlesex Hospital was an external member. I certainly claim no great mental abilities for my success; I was just very lucky in being asked the questions to which I knew the answers. The Pass in French was due to my failure in the oral examination. I had practised saying: "Monsieur, je suis un peu de sourde" but when faced with the examiner most of my French vanished from my head and when he asked me my name, my age and what sort of weather we were having, I hardly recollected the first two, while the weather beat me completely – it was a dull, heavy sort of day, bad enough to describe in English, let alone French. Doubtless my written paper showed that I was not so complete a fool as the oral had suggested and the Pass was awarded.

It could easily have been the other way – all failures. This was the opinion of 'Dicky' Richards – the master mentioned in my first account who had asked me my name and I said I had no idea. When he heard that I was down for the School Certificate he began to laugh . . . finally he had to be helped from the classroom and made to lie down for half an hour with the curtains drawn.

The extraordinary thing about schoolmasters is that no schoolboy credits them with leading a normal life outside school hours. Come four o'clock or later if after school activities were involved and the staff all disappeared into a kind of limbo, to re-appear the next morning. I never imagined them having lifestyles such as my parents and their friends enjoyed. I took this up once with the former Archbishop of Canterbury, Lord Coggan and he agreed with me.

My school life was hum-drum. Most people apparently considered me to be slightly mad and occasionally round the bend and out of sight, yet I received enough kindness to keep me cheerful. In 1936 the dance tune of the hour was The Way You Look To-night and, as always, I could not catch the words from my record. Symes, a classmate, offered to take them down for me and he gave me a written copy next day. My understanding of the first verse was inaccurate, to say the least. It was not: 'I'll be and the Old Kent Road above you' but 'I'll be all a-glow just thinking of you'. In similar fashion, before I could read, I thought my father's dental practice was in Three Man Street and it was a surprise to find it was really Queen Anne Street.

But perhaps I did suggest eccentricity . . . Once I was walking up and down the corridor making noises such as Hah! Huh! Hough! After a few minutes the door of the masters' common room was flung violently open and Teddy Rider bounced out "What the hell do you think you are doing, Jack?" he demanded angrily. "Practising my scornful laugh, Sir", I explained. He shot back into the commonroom after staring at me in amazement. God knows what he told his colleagues.

In the first week of my entry to Merchant Taylors I encountered one master who was the terror of the school and we attended his classroom for a French lesson. His name was John Fryers, known as Johnnie and I could never forget my first lesson with him. Thankfully it was also my last since I was then moved down into Form Lower Fourth B, the authorities having decided that A was too much for my weak intellect. This lesson was not concerned with French at all, merely the class being terrorized into submissive silence. The slightest sound or movement from any member of Lower Fourth A was instantly detected by the irascible bird of prey on the platform. One lad in particular was so terrified by the attacks made on his increasingly nervous twitchings that I really believed he was going to faint from sheer fright. No one ever explained what lay behind his insensate bullying. In later years he occasionally joined the Manor end-of-term concerts and gave extremely funny monologues.

It was incumbent upon me to approach every new master and explain that I should sit in front of the class because of my deafness. The idea of approaching Johnnie after this terrifying forty minute ordeal filled me with pure liquid horror but it had to be done. As the rest of our class left the room I walked onto the platform, quaking in my shoes. I was only thirteen and a half and never in my life (nor since, come to that) had I met anyone who operated such a reign of terror. As I neared his desk he glanced up and barked: "Well – what do you want, boy?" I said my little spiel about being deaf and needing to sit in front of the class. Johnnie looked down at me. "Thank you very much for telling me." he said kindly. All the same it was a good job I left his class – had I not done so I would soon have been at the barbed wire again, that's for sure.

My first headmaster in 1933 was Spencer Leeson, then a layman but at the time of his early death he was Bishop of Peterborough and a likely Archbishop of Canterbury before the appointment of Geoffrey Fisher around 1947.

I found him completely terrifying although the opposite of John Fryers; he was always very quiet and possessed of an immense dignity. My first encounter with him was as a new boy; he had us all in the chapel, one by one. I went in, he was sitting in the priest's stall and he motioned me to sit besides him. He uttered three words. "Name? Kneel. Pray . . ." Our class master was late one morning and after a few minutes the usual bedlam started up. A figure suddenly appeared in the doorway – the Headmaster. There was absolute dead silence. Leeson looked round the class, his icy glance boring holes through everyone. He deduced the ringleader and said quietly: "Brown, a gentleman does not behave like that". Brown, a battle-scarred veteran of many a caning, went bright scarlet and shuffled his feet – speechless.

I have never made up my mind whether spending most of my schooldays as a boarder was a Good Thing or the reverse. I suppose it taught me independence plus a high degree of secretiveness. I think day schooling with a regular home life would have produced a more balanced personality and maybe less eccentric – as my family will have it. My youngest grandson, Thomas, at twelve is suspected of a mild form of it; 'lateral thinking' my wife calls it. But great grandfather William Holt married his cousin Mary Ann Brown Whittell and their son Arnold Holt married his cousin Clara Eliza Whittell. So maybe there is a queer strain lurking around.

Living only four miles away I spent a great deal of my free time at home. As long as I was back in The Manor by lighting up time no questions were asked – except at the beginning when I refused to play rugger or cricket. Friends often came home with me. I had my model electric railway in my outside room, there was airgun shooting and above all, the river at the bottom of our garden – a small branch of the Colne, the main river lay half a mile across the fields beyond our little stream.

Soon after our arrival at Colne Mead my father and I built our first boat, a square stern flat bottom rowing boat and later we were more ambitious and built a double bowed twelve footer. Later I bought a folding canoe from Selfridges for seven pounds ten shillings. It took two people, the front paddler had his body from the hips downward underneath the canvas decking, which meant knocking away the back rest and moving pretty smartly when it overturned. Further down our river we passed a watercress bed owned by an irascible grower we called Hoppy Payne. He hated us since he was convinced that our peaceful paddling past his watercress meant muddy silt floating upstream into his watercress and if around when we passed by, we were met with a screaming volley of oaths and threats, followed by large clods of earth hurtling past our heads – I don't ever remember being hit so his aim must have been very poor.

Falling into the river became quite a routine. My oldest friend Ann came once to introduce her new husband and I offered to take him on the river. We both fell in and walked back to the house dripping with weeds and water. We were met by an infuriated Ann who shouted: "My God, Michael, I might have known what would happen to poor Douglas if I let him go on the river with you!". They had been married on three pounds a week; it was not only Douglas' best suit but also his only suit. It was one of those times when I adopted a low profile . . .

Another time a medical school friend, Bill Fairburn came for the day. We took the canoe on the Hippodrome, a sailing and bathing lake, a former quarry, in Rickmansworth. We had paddled out to the centre of the lake when the canoe turned over. Our picnic gear went to the bottom and we could have followed it as well but we managed to escape from the canoe and swim to shore, towing the canoe behind us. I don't say that my entire life flashed before my eyes as I struggled to extricate myself from within the canoe while hanging upside down in the water, but I gained the impression that the projector and screen were being set up ready for the show . . .

My knowledge of French, painfully acquired over years of study, always proved completely useless in France. Even if I was able to scratch together a few mis-pronounced phrases, I never managed to understand the replies. One of my mother's Whittell aunts had married a Frenchman (another married a Swede) and she spoke good French, having lived with her aunt for a year near Biarritz. My father also spoke French and I remember him best in Rouen, where we had visited Joan of Arc's prison and seen the square where she was burnt. Outside her jail my father chatted to a local Frenchman and had the temerity to suggest that The Maid had not been burnt at all; a substitute had been burnt and she herself lived to a good age in obscurity. This produced a foaming torrent of invective from the local gentleman and they went at it hammer and tongs. I believe this theory is held by some people.

I suspect that it was a terror of my mother's that her tall son might be seduced by any French shop girl in sight and during a visit to Tangier this put the stopper on a budding friendship. I had clapped up acquaintance on Tangier beach with a black lady who invited me back to her hotel bedroom for a drink. My parents made sure they came with me – which resulted in a boring evening.

My five guinea American organ was a source of great joy to me and my – musical friends; I spent endless hours practising music to play later on the West Hythe and Rickmansworth church organs. I even tried to teach two friends who could not play at all. My favourite was Charmian and I tried to teach her If I Should Fall In Love Again. She made little progress but sitting side by side, pedalling up the wind supply and guiding her fingers tenderly over the keys passed happy moments. Except early in our friendship when I told her: "Charmaine, you will not play E flat" and she suddenly 'blew up' and yelled that her name was Charmian. Our daughter is also Charmian and has the same problem, also friends shorten it to 'Char'. Sadly, Charmian had Hodgkin's Disease (cancer of the lymphatic glands) and then there was no cure. I had been told, as a medical student, that she was destined for an early death and that despite treatment – X rays badly scarred her neck – I would not enjoy her friendship for long. She never realised this; Audrey and I attended her twenty- first birthday party and she was dead a few months later. I still possess her last letter, recommending Audrey to drink raspberry tea to ease the arrival of Nicholas in 1945 and how she was looking forward to staying with us outside Aylesbury.

In the summers of 1936 and 1937 my parents and I spent holidays in St Mawes Cornwall in August. My father hired a sailing craft on each occasion. (Once he owned a yacht, which he berthed in Southampton). We used to sail around the inlets and bays and up the rivers in the area. We sailed across to Falmouth round Pendennis Point under the castle. Beached on the rocks we found four German submarines, fully accessible at low tide. I clambered aboard two of them and went inside the hulks – it was very creepy! I took home a stopcock which got its revenge by cutting my finger to the bone.

During our 1991 visit to Cornwall I made inquiries about the submarines in a photographic shop and the assistant told me she had heard something about them, and would pass on my query to a friend, a local retired teacher and historian, who very kindly wrote, giving the history of the submarines and in return I sent him my two photographs depicted here to copy for his records of Falmouth.

Mr Peter Gilson said in his letter that he remembered the submarines before the last war, he used to swim round them and agreed the interiors were very creepy. He said that the German submarines were better than the British and after the 1918 war the navy brought six of them to Falmouth, together with a lifting vessel called 'Cyclops'. Two of the submarines were tested to destruction and still lie on the floor of the bay and the other four were carried in by 'Cyclops' and dumped on the rocks below the castle. During World War II they were blown up for their valuable non-ferrous metals and the remains are still there but only visible during a low spring tide and then you have to know where to look.

In 1918, some German submarines beached onto rocks under Pendennis Castle, Falmouth, which we photographed on a visit in 1936.

Above: *Our first boat, at Colne Mead (1934).*

Below: *Michael's beloved American organ (1935).*

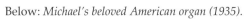

CHAPTER THREE

Middlesex Hospital Days

I entered the Middlesex in October 1938 and left it in June 1940 It was interrupted by the war, when the medical school went to Bristol for the autumn term and returned to London after Christmas. Having failed my First MB I was sent to a crammers near Victoria station and passed my first Conjoint exam. This is what my father had taken, qualifying as MRCS., LRCP.

I soon learnt to smoke, despite my father offering me five pounds if I did not smoke before I was twenty-one. The social pressure was too great; all the students in my year smoked and lit up after lectures and during practical work. I daresay smoking was a way of ridding oneself of the odour of formalin in the anatomy department. After weeks of saying No, I purchased a packet of ten Players Medium Navy Cut which set me back two and a half new pence – no filters! I smoked four in succession between Marylebone and Rickmansworth stations, a journey of forty five minutes. I cycled or walked the mile home to Mill End and collapsed into our Georgian loo – pale green, agonising pains and hoping the Angel of Death would put his head round the corner and offer to take me away with him.

As related earlier, our Professor of Anatomy was a Scotsman. We assembled in the Anatomy Department – to face twenty corpses laid out on trestle tables. I daresay it was the first time any of us had been in the presence of death and it was a chastening experience, even the noisiest students went quiet. The bodies did not seem to bear any relation to living people; I could not imagine them as individuals who had once been like me. For a start, they were several years old and had been through a process of embalming by the use of formalin, which has a most unpleasant smell that really gets up your nose. The bodies were a light tan in colour and completely shaved. They had been injected with dyes which turned the arteries and veins red and blue.

Professor Kirk instructed us in the routine of his classes; students paired off and were allotted an arm, a leg or whatever. The Professor told us severely that he expected us to behave better than his last class who had not only imbibed freely of beer during their classes but had even stood their beer bottles on the corpses. This, he said with a nasty Scotch glare, he would not tolerate again.

Slicing into the flesh was like cutting a ham or medium hard cheese. There could have been ten of us around each corpse and we had to dissect our portions down to the last nut and bolt. When the time came we detached our arm or leg from the body and at the end of the class dropped it into a huge tank of formalin, with a label on it. Next time in the department we had to fish around in this tank and find our bit of defunct humanity; one pulled up arms, legs, heads, bits of this and that. I don't recall anyone actually fainting in those classes but someone once slid to the floor in a dead faint during a physiology lecture involving a de-cerebrated cat.

We all possessed a skeleton or half skeleton for the study of the bones and attachment of muscles. My father bought me a half skeleton which included a complete skull and I kept it in a cardboard box under my bed. I proved quite good at bones and this came in useful in my churchyard levelling work, when I was bringing up bones and always managed to identify them. I used to carry my collection around without thinking about other peoples' reactions. This was brought home to me when I went to a dancing class in Baker Street and left my skull on the hall table. I was soon asked by the dance mistress to remove my skull – and me with it – because it was giving the girls such shocks that some had to go home immediately; I had been wondering what the screaming was about!

An incident which remains very clear is the time we were waiting for a physiology lecture from Professor Sammy Wright and some of us wandered out onto the flat roof. This had a skylight and looking down through it we saw a post mortem in progress. There was a horribly thin body – like those in concentration camps – sitting in a large dish filled with blood and some of the organs. As we watched the operator, he took a scalpel and ran it along the hairline above the eyebrows and then proceeded to pull the skin downwards . . . leaving a head without a face. This 'turned off' one or two students who had to go and sit down.

But I faced a lot of difficulty understanding what the anatomy demonstrators were saying as they visited each set of students. I began to question the whole basis of what had always been the end product of my education – qualifying as a doctor then perhaps going on to dentistry to join my father in his practice. I began to drift away, cutting lectures, trying church organs, meeting Ann and visiting the cinemas and exhibitions. It meant that after we all assembled at the hospital in 1940 I was so far behind the other members of my year that I became too discouraged to carry on – I had never even finished my arm dissection when my fellow student had passed his examination. After twenty years of a single goal in life it all proved a delusion.

My father was very good about my defection but my mother was dreadfully disappointed. It must have been May when I left the Middlesex and I remained at home until October, working on a farm near our house. The war was in progress of course and my father and I were members of the Home Guard. By virtue of his first war service he was immediately made a captain and I served as a private, without a uniform or a rifle. Later in the summer our group received a few rifles but no ammunition for them! I was guarding the local water works one night from eleven to three o'clock in the morning armed with a rifle but nothing to fire! The Germans were bombing London and from Mill End we could see the flames reflected in the sky as London burnt. The only exercise in which I took part was helping to dig a slit trench by the main Rickmansworth to Uxbridge road. We excavated down to four feet and uncovered the large gas main! Shades of Dad's Army; my father refused to watch this programme because he said it poked fun at a fine body of men.

We moved to London when the war broke out and we lived in rooms above the practice – which had fallen off considerably and was barely paying its way due to the fear of bombing raids on the city. I saw a lot of the routine at Number Eleven and heard about my father's patients but it left me without any particular wish to enter the firm. Film stars were among his patients – for instance John Laurie – Private Fraser of Dad's Army. He had some teeth taken out once and when he recovered from the anaesthetic and started talking said: "My God, I've lost my Scotch accent!". He had not, of course.

One of old Queen Mary's ladies in waiting expressed the hope that 'our dear Queen will come to you, Mr Jack' but she never did. I am sure my father was relieved; he would not have wanted the hassle involved with royalty. I know my mother was deeply disappointed and she put it all down to The Golf Club.

I was outside Number Eleven one morning when a large Daimler drew up outside the house. It had no number plates so I knew royalty was involved. The chauffeur opened the door and the old Queen Mother appeared. I knew she was not a patient and she must be visiting the well known antique dealer at Number Nine. Sure enough, the Queen crossed the pavement towards his house and there I was, quite by myself, faced with the terrifying sight of the Queen Mother coming towards me! What should I do? As she passed by I gave a deep bow and received a gracious inclination of her head. Her dignity and royal presence were so terrific that after she had disappeared next door I could have rolled into the gutter and barked like a dog.

In keeping with his independent character my father stood no nonsense from his patients. The Minister of Transport in the Conservative government, Leslie Hore-Belisha, was a patient. (He left us his legacy of Belisha Beacons). His secretary rang up one morning and told my father's receptionist Pam that Mr. Hore-Belisha would be along at three o'clock' to have his teeth checked.

"Tell him he can't come", said my father sharply. "He must make an appointment like everyone else". The Minister never came again!

There was also the time when a female patient invited my father to fondle her bosom. He was always careful to keep his receptionist in the surgery when he had females in the chair. He was a good looking, charming and very amusing man and I am sure many of his ladies would have enjoyed having more than their teeth inspected. This time he was quite taken aback but the lady insisted he fondled her breast so he extended a cautious forefinger and gave a gentle prod. "What do you think of that, Mr. Jack? It's rubber – nearly all of it!".

After my decision to give up medicine my father sent me to an industrial psychologist, hoping to find out where my ability to earn a living (if any) might lie. I submitted to two hours of written, oral and manual dexterity tests. A long report arrived, confirming that medicine was not in my best interests (in which deafness was probably a deciding factor). It suggested some form of outdoor life would be better, lessening my dependence on social contacts and making use of my mechanical ability – such as farming. The psychologist also gave me an extremely high Intelligence Quota which came as a complete surprise to everybody, including me. It shows that experts can always make mistakes.

ATTENDING WEDDINGS

Above: *Mother and self at the wedding of the British Museum's Head Librarian's daughter, Wilma Keon-Boyd, 1935. Michael recalls another occasion when he attended lunch in Mr. Keon-Boyd's apartments at the British Museum. He was waited upon by a footman standing behind, attending to his every need, but felt very intimidated as he was unsuitably dressed!* Above right: *Mother and Father at our wedding.*

My mother Vera, self , wife Audrey, Kathleen and Gerald, my father, on the way to a wedding (Kathleen had been my father's receptionist).

CHAPTER FOUR

The Appledore Farm

A patient of my father's who lived outside Aylesbury suggested a farming friend who might take me on as a farm pupil and in October 1940 I moved to Richard Rowland's Walton Court Farm outside Aylesbury near the Stoke Mandeville hospital, then run by the Middlesex Hospital. I have mentioned how I met a land girl, Audrey Richardson and married her three and a half years later. After two years I left the Rowland farm and moved to Geoff Norman's Manor Farm at Rowsham, four miles out of Aylesbury on the Leighton Buzzard road. When he heard we were getting married, Geoff offered me one of his farm cottages at a rental of three shillings weekly (15p) and kindly let me spend much of the winter decorating the interior. The rent included free milk, we kept chickens, had a large allotment and later had bees and kept pigs. We grew half a ton of maincrop potatoes with the farm crop and really ate very well; farm workers had extra rations – double summertime was in operation and we were often haymaking and harvesting until ten at night, with milking starting at 6.30 in the morning.

With unlimited milk we were able to make butter from the cream and eggs were so plentiful we were able to sell a few to increase our income which was a basic three pounds fifty when we were married plus overtime at haymaking and harvest. Compared to many townees we lived very well – my mother's brother Toddy Holt was by then a Lieut-Colonel in the Royal Army Service Corps (he had been in tanks in the first war) and my aunt told us that they practically starved in the war.

Our home was a good one, as farm cottages went. We had a small hall opening off a front porch, a sitting room with a kitchen behind, which had a copper in one corner and three smaller rooms upstairs. We had mains electricity for lighting and cooking – our Jackson cooker cost us £24 in 1944 and we used it until we finally left Biddenden in 1958. It was in good working order and fetched 25p at a local auction sale – less commission.

We bought a long tin bath in Aylesbury and hung it outside on the back wall of our cottage. We heated water in the copper, stood the bath on the stone kitchen floor and ladled the hot water into the bath. The water was hot but our bottoms curiously cold.

Sanitary arrangements were of the old fashioned country kind, a brick-built outside loo up the garden path with a 'one holer' inside. Our Georgian home in Mill End had a similar arrangement outside the kitchen but was a 'two holer'. Underneath was a bucket which was emptied when necessary into trenches dug across the back garden. It was perfectly satisfactory – as it had been for generations and the only time we found it inconvenient was after we had been reading Bram Stoker's Dracula. It frightened us so much that neither of us would venture down the path alone after dark. While one went inside the other kept guard outside, just in case Dracula took it into his head to pay us a visit. The only thing that ever startled me was our cat, which came in and jumped on my lap while I was dozing on the seat with the door open, basking in the sunshine.

I mentioned earlier our famous old Baby Austin Leonard. I did not mention how Audrey learnt to drive him. She did not, really, the lesson was a disaster. At the end of our lane was the main road between Aylesbury and Leighton Buzzard. Audrey set off down the slope towards the road in bottom gear. Having been driving in cars all my life I did not realise that Audrey had absolutely no knowledge of cars at all, beyond how to sit in the passenger seat. I explained about the gears, how to steer and the clutch but I never told her how to stop the car! Consequently as we neared the main road Audrey began asking me how to stop. I told her to press down the brake pedal, not realising I might as well have been speaking in Greek. We rolled slowly over the road at a walking pace and crashed into a brick wall on the other side. This had been finished only two days earlier by the owner and the entire length of wall fell over on its side. The owner bounced out of his front door, registering horror and dismay. I had the insurance cover note but the premium had not been fixed, nevertheless the National Farmers Union paid without a quibble. Rebuilding the wall cost £ 11.13s.6d.

Nicholas had arrived in March 1945 and Nigel was expected in May 1947. My mother decided we could not possibly have two young children in our farm cottage and we must have a farm of our own. We went around the country seeking a suitable farm to rent and eventually chose the Appledore farm. The terms on which we were asked to take over were most unsatisfactory from our point of view and had still to be resolved when the landlord sent a telegram to say he was taking over a new business the following week and would we take over immediately. So willy nilly I was pitchforked into the new venture in one of the worst winters on record. It is still quoted when hard winters are mentioned – that of 1947. It started in mid-February and continued unabated until the end of March. We were to face considerable difficulties without the appalling weather and it left us in financial straits from which we never recovered.

I set off from Rowsham in thick snowfall and a hard frost, spent the night with my uncle in Sutton, Surrey and arrived in Appledore the following afternoon with a suitcase and a crate containing three laying fowls and a cockerel in the back. Leonard was a 1931 model; looking back on that epic drive I simply cannot imagine how I was brave enough to make the journey. I took over the farm on 23rd February and celebrated my 27th birthday alone in the village, staying in the Red Lion nearby. Audrey and Nicholas came down with my parents two days later with the furniture. Audrey's brother Philip was a Lancaster bomber pilot in the war and had started on the Aylesbury Farm Institute on demobilisation; he gave it up to join us in Appledore.

In late May I took Audrey back to Aylesbury Hospital to have baby Nigel. This was another extraordinary journey. We collected a puncture within ten yards of the farm house. It took eight hours to do the journey because we became lost somewhere after Cranbrook [we had not then heard of the A20] and ended up driving through the wilds of Bromley, and even managing to pass the HMV gramophone record factory in Hayes, Essex.

We encountered immense difficulties at once mostly due to the freezing conditions and lack of proper farm transport. We milked five cows on the farm and ran twenty-five 'followers' down on The Dowels a mile away and across two fields belonging to another farmer. In all Romney Marsh The Dowels were the lowest land below sea-level; they were covered in poor quality grass and rushes and in summer a plentiful crop of thistles. Now there was a foot of snow on the grazing so the cattle needed a daily feed of hay and cattle nuts. We had nothing to convey the bulky hay down to the cattle. We had the farm tractor but that was frozen into the mud in the market garden. We managed to get it started and then came the business of getting the tractor on the road – the wheels had spade lugs and to make it roadworthy we had to jack up each wheel in turn and bolt on a series of curved wooden blocks between the lugs – this took an hour. Having driven down to the Dowels entrance gate we had to dismantle the road blocks (no grip on the snow was possible with the smooth wood surfaces). The cattle were then fed, tractor driven back to the road and the blocks bolted on again. An utterly frenetic time-wasting bad tempered operation. The answer lay in the Tamkin road bands which we soon bought and I have described earlier. Later I bought a set of tractor wheels with rubber tyres.

Starting up the tractor was enough to drive anyone into a mental home. In cold weather the sheer effort of turning over the engine with the starting handle left us exhausted – no electric starter on those wartime Fordsons! When eventually it fired, it was impossible to get it into gear because the entire contents of the gearbox appeared to turn in a solid mass. Any attempt to ease the gear lever into first gear resulted in a horrendous grating and clashing which could be heard all over our end of the village. One result of this was that our Vicar would never allow Philip to drive the Vicarage motor, fearing he might do to his gears what he had heard him doing on the tractor! Occasionally I found it necessary to flog the tractor with a piece of knotted rope in an effort to persuade it to start.

During the weeks of frosty weather the cattle became accustomed to walking on the ice in the dykes and when the thaw started we lost several animals from drowning. About this time a Distress Fund had been set up to help farmers in financial difficulties due to the hard winter. I went over to Stone, the next village, where our MP lived to ask for funds. This was E.P. Smith our Ashford MP who wrote plays under the name of Edward Percy – The House at Sly Corner was made into a film. He was able to obtain a grant but only for four cattle since the Agricultural Committee decided some of the blame must be laid on the terms we had hastily negotiated with our landlord. Incidentally E.P. Smith was the gentleman who introduced the Romney Marsh frogs into the area. They escaped from his pond and spread all over the Marsh. Even I could hear their call during the mating season – a monotonous Koax! Koax! Koax! I daresay they are still around and a walk alongside most dykes is accompanied by a continual plopping as the extra large frogs dive into the water from the bank.

We fed the livestock to the best of our limited ability but we had taken over very little food with the farm and except for hay, straw and roots the concentrated foodstuffs were on coupons. We had to buy in hay and straw which further depleted my limited financial resources. Then a well meaning local lady reported us to the RSPCA! Our local police officer brought an Inspector from the Society to the farm and we went over the holding with him and down to The Dowels, explaining the situation. The verdict was that we were blameless, caught up in conditions beyond our control. Everyone in the village knew of our plight and the general opinion was that we had been very foolish to take over the farm on the terms we did.

We were issued with extra coupons to increase the livestock rations – which was fine but the food had to be paid for, along with the seed corn and fertiliser for our thirteen acres rented a mile away at Munks Farm in the opposite direction to The Dowels. I started an overdraft from which we never recovered and calculating our losses when we left in the spring of 1953, I reckon we lost five hundred pounds annually. I had borrowed the money from my parents – £1,500 each – and eventually the sum came from my mother's Estate in 1960 and the other from my father's when he died in 1978.

After two or three head of cattle had drowned in the dykes we decided we would have to bring the survivors up to the home fields rented from a neighbour on a sub-tenancy. This involved driving them along the canal bank for a mile, along the main road to the centre of Appledore and finally down the farm lane. The cattle were weakened by the severe weather, several were in calf – at least one much too early in life and she started calving before we had made progress along the canal bank. We had no option but to leave her there and press on with the rest of the herd.

Having penned them in a field we telephoned our vet. in Rye who sent out his assistant. We disliked him at sight, a red-faced gentleman who seemed extremely put out at being called away. When he discovered that he would have to walk the best part of a mile along the snow-covered canal bank his colour deepened to an alarming puce and when he saw the calving heifer he turned an ugly purple and spoke about fools who allowed their cattle to be mated too young. We explained we had only recently taken over the farm but I think he considered us to be a couple of liars. The heifer was so weak she looked as if she might die during calving. However, 'Purple Face' (as we termed this gentleman) set to work on the prospective mother, sending me off for a small pole to act as a lever to ease out the calf. I floundered about in the mud, trying to retrieve a pole – actually one of those erected on The Marsh during the war to prevent enemy aircraft landing – and finally fell in, freezing mud squelching over the tops of my gum boots. Staggering back, I flung down my pole and emptied out my footwear, thus giving Philip his first laugh for three days.

The vet. merely grunted, obviously thinking that a fool who allowed his cattle to be mated too early was just the type to fall into the mud.

The herd began to recover but six of them died and we hauled them up to the road behind the tractor for the knacker's lorry to collect the corpses. I received between a pound and thirty shilling per animal. Apart from feeding problems and deaths the cattle were natural escapologists. They were never satisfied and no matter where we put them they always wanted to be elsewhere. They became experts on breaking out; the state of the farm hedges and fences left much to be desired. We checked every field before putting in the cattle and we reckoned that even an elephant could not escape. But they possessed a huge store of cunning. Put them in a new field and we would note their eyes darting this way and that, seeking a weak spot in the defences – perhaps a post where I had hammered my thumb instead of the wire staple. Once we had left, the cattle went carefully over every inch of the perimeter and having found a weak spot they then pushed one of their number through the potential opening. This was usually Minnie and if ever a cow was missing it was sure to be Minnie. Thin and slinky looking, she was sent out as a scout and if she failed to return then the rest of the herd broke out – nothing stopped them. Even wide dykes full of water which penned in ordinary cattle were no obstacle, wading through muddy slime up to their back axles.

Time and time again our neighbours rang us at all hours of the day – and night: "Mr. Jack, your cows have broken out again . . ." The most painful occasion was being woken up at midnight by the village policeman, who had heard curious thumping sounds coming from the churchyard while he was patrolling past. Our cows were grazing down the churchyard jungle. We hastily dressed and tried to drive the miscreants back through the hole in the hedge. As usual this did not work because they could never find their way back by the same route. Chasing around the gravestones is not a memory I cherish. The artful animals could see better in the dark than we could and dodged the obstacles leaving us to fall over curbstones or bark our shins on low railings. We could almost hear them laughing heartily as they trotted about.

The next crisis arose because our landlord had sublet the fields nearest the farm from the landlord of the Red Lion who had not been told of the sub-tenancy and gave our landlord notice to quit. (Eventually he built himself a house on one of the fields). These ten acres were a vital part of our dairy farm and without them the milking was not a viable proposition at all. We should have sued our landlord for breach of contract; it is a mystery to me why we never did so. Instead, we tried to carry on the dairy by renting a stretch of the bank along the Royal Military Canal from Appledore towards Rye. This was rough grazing and poor quality grass, much of it under the shade of the fine Elm trees (which succumbed to Elm Tree Disease in the 1970's). The bank was bounded by the canal on one side – which even our cows never tried to cross – and a five strand wire fence on the road side. This might have contained normal cattle but to our practised Houdinis it was literally a walk over! We had to erect a one strand electric fence operated by a high voltage shocking coil every second or so; the wire ran over ceramic insulators. Philip used to test it by laying a finger on the wire and if he gave a sharp howl and jumped in the air we knew it was working. Curiously, I never tested it myself. Our bull Willie Moo Moo was once on the bank and gave the wire an exploratory sniff; his copper ring touched the wire and all four of his feet left the ground with the shock! But people would deliberately short the wire, thereby earthing it and draining the battery. The bank grazing was more trouble than it was worth. At least once I had gone down to bring up the cows for early morning milking and found them walking halfway to Rye.

We then moved the milkers to Munks Farm where our previous cornfields were down for hay. It meant loading up Leonard twice a day with hay, cattle nuts and dairy equipment. We set down the rations in front of each cow in turn and they placidly munched away while we milked them. Then they resumed their bad old ways and started breaking out again. I finally gave up the struggle and sold the lot to a local farmer who wanted them to suckle calves. We retained one cow –

Stewart – which he would not take at any price, had her tuberculin tested (which by some extraordinary freak she passed), and kept her as a house cow. How she became drunk on windfall apples and her eventual fate I have related elsewhere.

It was a relief not running the milking business. The monthly cheque from the Milk Marketing Board was useful but had we costed the profits they must have been small, with all the running about between canal bank or fields. In fact I must confess that nothing was properly assessed for the profit level and we never knew exactly how the accounts stood except that at the end of the year the overdraft was larger and there was no profit for the income tax to collect, according to my accountant. We no longer faced the spectre of the milk lorry driver coming down the lane screaming with fury because we had not finished cooling the milk in time.

The landlord had built a substantial concrete block asbestos roofed milking parlour with a yard attached, bounded by the wartime Fire Station on one side and a concrete block wall on the other. A cattle lorry backed down the lane one morning and as the driver climbed out of his cab his door just touched the wall. The whole caboodle then fell over on its side in one solid mass. The driver surveyed it open-mouthed and muttered feebly: "Honest, Guv'nor, I 'ardly touched it!" The reason was soon apparent; the mortar binding the blocks together was mostly pure sand. Philip re-built the wall but unfortunately he had not realised that vertical joints are staggered and he built it with the joints running from bottom of the wall to the top which gave it a slightly bizarre appearance. At least it never fell down again.

Besides the dairy herd we had some bullocks and yearlings – as well as Willie Moo Moo the bull. nine yearlings went to a spring sale of stock and made good prices. Two bullocks ate a lot of food but did not gain much weight so we booked them into Ashford market as 'fat stock'. Ashby's cattle truck backed into the yard, the driver let down the ramp but nothing would persuade those bullocks to enter the truck – peculiar, like all the rest of the livestock. We managed to lassoo one bullock by its horns and with a combination of pulling and shoving got it up into the truck. The driver at the end of the rope then foolishly passed it through the slatted side of the truck to me outside. I immediately pulled it tight, thereby trapping the driver between the bullock and the side of the truck.

"Oi", he yelled. "I'll 'ave to cut the bloody rope!". The thought of the bullock escaping from the lorry galvanised Philip into action and he shambled rapidly round to the ramp and shut both bullock and driver in the truck. We stuffed hay through the slats, whereupon the bullock started eating the hay and we were able to release the driver, by then a sickly grey colour. "Cor!", he complained bitterly: "That's done zummat to me, that'as!". The other bullock trotted up into the truck on seeing its

30

mate eating hay. It was then quite late and at lunch time Ashbys rang up and delivered a rocket for the delay in getting the truck to market – holding up all the other farmers after us.

At half past six we saw the same truck backing down the lane; the ramp was lowered and before our horrified eyes those terrible bullocks trotted nimbly down the ramp – home again! Rejected as fatstock – not surprising – we re-entered them the following week as 'store cattle' and gained a good price. Whether their new owner succeeded in fattening them up I took good care not to find out.

With the departure of Willie Moo Moo we needed the services of a neighbouring bull up the road. The time came and I put a halter round Stewart's neck to lead her gently along – she was a placid animal. But once in the village street she had other ideas and set off at a fast trot, turning down a side lane into a garden and back up to the road again, pausing only to deposit an enormous cow pat in the centre of a clump of rhubarb. (I imagined the house wife complaining to her husband:" Really Joe, you could have waited until you were indoors").

We made cream and butter from Stewart's surplus milk and bought supplies from a local farmer who ran a dairy herd of Jersey cows, when Stewart was not in milk.

Included in the livestock was a peculiar little beast we called The Heirloom. Small, but looking quite ancient, she had a thin curly coat, two tiny horns and a vacant eye. One day she completely vanished and we never saw her again. From time to time we heard vague rumours that she had been sighted several miles away but we did not bother about her and merely wondered if she had achieved some kind of levitation – she looked that sort of animal.

The author with his brother Philip in 1945. Philip was a bomber pilot in the RAF.

MY WIFE AND I

Above left: *Audrey at Aylesbury, pre-war and* (right) *as a Land Army Girl in 1941.*

Michael and Audrey at Aylesbury (1943).   *Also at Appledore about 1950.*

Right:
Military Canal Bank.

Above:
Cattle grazing on Romney Marsh.

Right:
Dead Cattle after the epic march from the marshes in the severe winter of 1947.

Left:
Fire station and pigsties at Clifton House.

CHAPTER FIVE

Pigs

The farm livestock included nine fattening Saddleback pigs and a large sow we named Massiva, who featured in the earlier book. I mentioned how Massiva grew larger and fatter, being supposedly in-pig. Eventually we decided to take her to a boar a mile up the road towards Tenterden and we walked her gently along to the boar's sty where he did his business and we walked her home again. It transpired later that the excellent material so heartily supplied by the boar must have dropped out at the back on the way home – we had another long wait for nothing. This time we selected a Tamworth boar which lived a good deal further away, so we placed Massiva in the farm trailer, attached it to Leonard and set off. Baby Austins had many excellent qualities but they had not been designed by the makers to haul trailers containing large fat pigs; consequently we moved slowly along in second gear. Just before reaching our destination, Leonard seemed to find the going easier and we stopped to see if the trailer had become unhitched. It was still behind Leonard but a part of the floor had vanished. From being a passenger Massiva had become an active partner. Her front feet were on the trailer but she had been walking smartly along on her hind trotters. This time there was no mistake and Massiva produced a litter of Tamworth Saddlebacks. Alas! It would be too painful to relate their fate again.

The original baconers were sold off at eight to ten score deadweight – 160 to 200 pounds weight. Besides their bought rations (from Pledges the Ashford millers), we boiled up kitchen refuse collected from around the village on Saturday mornings in a queer old water tank on wheels. It rumbled along sounding like a tumbril in the French Revolution carrying the aristocracy to the guillotine. Once home, Philip lit a fire in the boiler, the steam from this passed into a pressure cooker into which he loaded the pig swill and anything available on the farm, which could include unsold vegetables, fruit and even the odd animal which had handed in its cards. The resultant aroma was not one would expect say, in the royal kitchens. This boiler had reputedly blown up the previous year, demolishing its little shed and sending up the iron chimney pipe like a rocket. We had been warned that it could always happen again – which it did not but it made the operations more interesting. Philip used rotten old bean poles to keep up a ferocious fire but he kept down the steam pressure.

We bought weaner pigs in Ashford market and did quite well fattening them up; we retained one baconer for ourselves. We took it over the road to our local butcher and later he delivered two fine sides of bacon, hams, sausages and other porcine delights. We green cured the bacon by rubbing in, among other things, saltpetre, common salt and black treacle. In return we gave up our bacon rations for a period but while we had the pig meat we lived like lords.

This gave a local lady the idea that she also could benefit from killing a pig and joined in with us to keep one with ours, supplying the swill – and not much else as I recall. When I first called at her house it was all 'dear Mr. Jack' and the best sherry. After the episode had ended I was lucky to be given thin beer and we parted company. The lady was greedy and wanted a larger pig than was economic. We had these two pigs in one sty; the time came when I said our pig was going to the butcher and she said her pig must be fattened up even further. Left on its own her pig began to pine and started losing weight. She had to give in but the return on her bacon rations was nothing like she had hoped for! She complained loudly and bitterly.

Milkman *Milk maid*

Selling fruit and vegetables on the roadside at Clifton House.

CHAPTER SIX

Chickens

The livestock included eighty-four laying fowls, six ducks, nine geese and a gander. The ducks were picked off one by one by rats. My uncle Guy Holt was staying with us when the last duck was found horribly mauled and dead. Uncle rushed to tell us the awful news and was astonished when Philip and I merely laughed. The chickens laid some eggs but spent much of their time dying. There was a foot of snow in the orchard; this, and the poor quality of the food we had taken over with the farm was not sufficient nourishment. In spite of feeding them morning and evening, a bird taken to Wye College for a post mortem examination was declared to have died from starvation! By then the RSPCA had gained us extra rations and the flock began to improve; egg production went up and there were no more deaths.

In April Philip and I drove Leonard to Lydd and bought a hundred day old chicks. Once again things did not do well and we reared barely ten per cent of them. The following year we bought eight week old pullets which proved very successful. With the sale of the milking herd I bought four portable chicken houses which we moved around the orchard and the field we rented below the churchyard. The cowshed being empty we turned it into a deep litter house and altogether we ran about two hundred birds. They were lorded over by Alfred, the cockerel who had journeyed down from Rowsham with me. His wives sometimes wandered off to secluded places and later turned up followed by clusters of baby chicks.

Disaster struck yet again after we had built a hen house out of straw bales with a corrugated roof in the orchard and installed twenty-five pullets, coming into lay. Philip went in one morning to release and feed the birds and found them all with their throats torn open, lying on the floor, blood spattered everywhere. As we looked at the slaughter Philip grabbed my arm. "I think there is something moving under the floor", he whispered. He went off and came back with a pick-axe and a shovel. I pulled up the tin sheeting to reveal a white ferret sleeping off its

37

debauchery. Quick as a flash, Philip's shovel descended and flattened the criminal.

In much the same way the first chickens we reared began to vanish and we found only wing feathers in the orchard. Keeping watch, we found it was three wild cats abandoned by their owners, living rough nearby. I got out my shot gun and set about shooting them, picking them off within three days. The last cat was lurking by the black currant bushes and just as I was about to fire, Philip came round the corner, spoiling my aim. The cat escaped on that occasion but I cut down two currant bushes and smashed three panes of greenhouse glass. The day after this happened an old lady called to ask if I had seen her cat. I said I had not but would keep an eye open for it. She hesitated and then blurted out: "Oh Mr. Jack you won't shoot him, will you?" Thank goodness her cat turned up soon afterwards or its disappearance would have been laid at my door.

We sold six of the original geese for two pounds each, keeping the gander and two geese. There was no mistaking the gander, who was white, his wives were grey. He resented everybody but was a coward and as soon as someone had passed by he came rushing up, hissing like a soda syphon. I failed to hear him coming once and he landed on my shoulder but was so surprised to find himself there that he fell off. He would even attack Leonard as he passed through the orchard. Most of all he waged unrelenting warfare against the two small boys who were more his size. The old gander once knocked down Nigel and stalked up and down his back, pecking at his posterior while Nicholas tried to beat him off with a stick. A year before we left the farm, Nicholas then being seven, he gained his revenge for years of terrorism and gave the gander a good beating, which cured him of attacking all and sundry.

Every year the geese laid fertile eggs and produced baby goslings, enchanting little creatures. We had to give them to broody hens to rear as the geese proved hopeless mothers. Their favourite trick was to lead them into thickets of rough grass and nettles, leaving the babies to find their own way out – which sometimes they did not and later we found the little corpses. Or the mothers got all excited over nothing at all and trampled their offspring to death – later reminding me of Corporal Jones in Dad's Army and his Don't panic! Don't panic!

One gosling was white and grew into a good bird; we wondered if it was a gander. In the village we had a self-proclaimed expert on geese – knew everything about geese, he did. It is very difficult to tell the sex of a goose from looking at it. (Now I suppose someone will write and say it is perfectly easy.) Just give him the bird and he would tell us the sex. So we caught the bird, handed it over and the Expert turned it round and about, looked at its beak, peered into its eyes, examined its keel, sniffed its breath and finally came up with his verdict: "Ho yes it's a gander!" Next season the gander laid a clutch of eggs. The Expert was unabashed.

"Ah well, it were a young 'un, you know. Very 'ard to tell with young 'uns".

When my mother-in-law came to live in Appledore Philip moved into her house, about a hundred yards from our lane and the geese took to walking along to their house at six in the morning. This made them somewhat unpopular with some of the villagers since they kept up a prodigious hissing and honking. But no one really minded since their stately procession looked so amusing. Not as bad as a neigbouring farmer's peacocks which sat on the rooftops shrieking their heads off.

We sold a popular line in caponised cockerels for the Christmas trade, home reared birds on totally free range in the orchard. These birds possessed a superb flavour and weighed from eight to ten pounds. The method of caponising was to inject a small pellet under the skin of one leg of each bird, using a hypodermic syringe of special construction. This slowly dissolved in the next few weeks and effectively smothered the cockerel's male characteristics.

Philip held each bird with one leg held out ready for me to insert the point of the syringe under the loose skin and press down the plunger. One bird began to struggle and Philip's hand slipped at the exact moment I started injecting into the leg and it was only some nifty hand work that enabled me to avoid setting the pellet under Philip's skin! We wondered what the result would have been; perhaps he would have started speaking with a squeaky voice!

Our chickens were fed on the normal rations of hard corn – usually wheat – and a mixture of other products such as flaked maize and ground foodstuffs which we mixed up on the concrete floor and bagged up each month after Pledges had delivered the order. There was a lot of waste from the market garden; some was boiled up with the pig swill and the smaller items were fed into a mechanical cutter operated by an electric motor. It shredded everything into small pieces – apples, pears, potatoes, runner beans for example and this was mixed daily into the poultry rations. The eggs were collected weekly by Stonegate Farmers.

The chickens were Philip's province which covered quite a wide area. An old hen house in the orchard held seventy laying fowls; they had the run of the two and a half acre orchard. Another forty or so birds lived on deep litter in the former cowshed after the milking herd had been sold; we scattered a bale of straw when needed. The litter went on the manure heap beyond the fire station, plus the cow manure and bedding and that from the pig sties. It all went up to the market garden conveyed in Leonard. Another 4 score birds lived in the four hen houses in the field below the church. They were on free range and we moved the houses in regular fashion across the field.

At one time I tended eight bee hives in the orchard and we had honey for sale – I managed to eat around half a pound of honey a day. The honey combs were taken to the wash house behind the kitchen and the honey extracted with a hand operated centrifuge. Many thousands of bees converged on the vicinity anxious to reclaim their honey. It became a no-go area for all our customers, unable to face the tremendous humming and the air black with determined bees. While mowing the orchard I knocked over a bee hive and there was an angry reaction from the inmates. I just ran for my life and reached the back door before the first bees hurled themselves against the glass panels. For good measure I bolted it top and bottom and thus defeated even the Appledore bees.

CHAPTER SEVEN

Farm Routine

Occasionally I have mentioned our farm truck, Leonard, which was renowned throughout the entire neighbourhood, after we had cut him in half with two hacksaws. The first platform was a shaky affair supported by two angle irons resting on the back axle and tied on with wire. Coming down from the market garden one morning, I glanced round and was amazed to see the platform had disappeared, being halfway up the lane with Beetle Dog still sitting on it – he was an Australian terrier. He was a sharp witted dog and did not walk if he could be transported. He once slyly eased a packet of chocolate from my pocket, stripped off the paper and ate the contents before I noticed my loss.

Our radio set lived up to the queerness of the farm while the sound production became worse and worse and an inspection inside the innards showed that three quarters of the loudspeaker cone had been eaten by a mouse. We introduced Beetle to the radio. he sniffed, stiffened and pounced and caught that mouse.

Later on our blacksmith welded on a substantial sheet metal body and we used Leonard to convey all the farm produce from the market garden to the former wartime fire station, our store and packing shed. His large wheels and high construction enabled him to go anywhere on the farm, even in muddy conditions. He carried up the three thousand or so runner bean poles we stuck in every year for the bean crop – Appledore stick beans were renowned in the locality and London markets and most farmers grew them. He took boxes down to Appledore station a mile away if the wholesale lorry was not available and he went to Hastings – until a policeman who saw him at Appledore station observed that I would certainly be hanged if I was spotted in Ashford; thereafter I confined his activities to the village. Until that painful business which ended in the magistrates' court in Ashford which really would be too awful to relate again.

In October 1947 I bought a Standard Flying Nine but even this was not immune from disasters. We were setting off to Rye one morning and

The original "Leonard", our Baby Austin.

Leonard "converted".

toddler Nicholas was left alone in the car for a few minutes. When we came back, he had taken off the hand brake and the car had rolled back into the hedge. We drove off but then there was a crunching sound from behind the car; it had rolled back on to Nicholas' tricycle and squashed it flat. Thinking about that kept the little lad quiet for several miles.

On the whole the boys were very good. The only really naughty thing I remember is when they turned on the tractor paraffin oil tap on the two hundred gallon tank and overcome by panic they rushed away. I happened to enter the garage not long afterwards but not before about sixty gallons had been lost. On that occasion I did more than lift my finger and say Tweet Tweet!

There was a funeral at the church only a few yards from our farm and as the procession turned into the churchyard gates our Vicar's wife came by shopping. Bringing up the rear of the mourners following the coffin she saw two entirely naked little boys – naked, that is, except for their gumboots. Horrified, she grabbed hold of them and brought them back to the farm. An interesting speculation – what would have happened had the boys actually entered the church? Our elderly Vicar might have coped since just before our arrival in the village he had actually found a naked woman in the church. He devised some kind of a formula and drove her home in the next village, explaining to her husband he had brought her back – this was a regular occurrence.

I cannot resist interpolating a story about Wye churchyard which took place many years later when I was rotary mowing the back churchyard. An acquaintance stopped me at the gate and asked if I was aware that a girl had taken up residence in the churchyard, sleeping outside if fine and in the porch if it was wet. Furthermore – he sank his voice to a whisper – the congregation had been scandalised because she had been seen sunbathing naked among the tombstones. I said I had no idea but would go round and see if she was all right, at which my informant gave a sharp cackle and walked away. I found her in the cemetery discreetly if skimpily dressed and bought her an ice cream. Next time Audrey and I were mowing we shared our coffee with her.

However, I digress. Another farm activity I started was a greengrocery round in the village, using an old Morris van. By this time my father had retired from Queen Anne Street to a farm on the outskirts of Woodchurch, four miles away. This venture was to be a joint affair but before it got off the ground we had a furious row with my father over how to run it and he never came to our farm again for a year. He himself had also been a "spoilt only child" in Putney and liked having his own way. We had always sold fruit, vegetables, eggs and honey from the farm and built up a good little trade so the travelling van was an extension of this. Philip and I loaded the van twice weekly with farm produce, supplemented with wholesale items and visited most homes in Appledore. A big drawback was the time wasted in consuming refreshment kindly offered by our customers. Everyone knew I had been a medical student and I was constantly asked for advice. One pretty and plump young mother asked me about her sore nipples due to breast feeding her baby. I gave her my ideas on the subject and moved on to the next customer. It then struck me I should have asked her to trot out her nipples and given her even better advice after a careful inspection.. But by then I was transacting a sale in bananas. Opportunities like that are quite rare.

I really did not enjoy touting my wares but as we knew everybody in the village it was not like trying to sell insurance to strangers. We had one very glamorous lady who lived up a side lane, so Philip and I were together when we called on her. She came out of her cottage with what I called her 'practised walk' meaning as an actress but she pretended referred to a much older profession. Her personality and humour put us in such a tizzy neither Philip nor I could added up her bills and she kindly did it for us.

Another customer lived nearby in a 16th century cottage, a heavily timbered and tile-hung property with the rain leaking through the roof in several places. This lady was slightly eccentric, wearing green earplugs in winter and brown ones in summer. She played a harmonium in the sittingroom which was surrounded by buckets to catch the rain dripping down. At the back of the house was an equally ancient tiled barn which one morning she said was falling down. I gave it a slap and said it was good for many years. The barn took instant umbrage; two minutes later there was a cracking and groaning and it collapsed in front of us into a heap of rubble.

In 1952 it was obvious our farming days in Appledore were numbered. Philip moved into estate. agency work in Ashford. I carried on the farm and the vegetable round by myself for a while and then a friend offered to buy it from me. we agreed on a figure of twelve pounds for the good will and he came round with me twice, getting to know the customers. When the morning came to go on his own he had cold feet, unable even to make a start and he had another travelling greengrocer to take over my customers. But he insisted on paying me the twelve pounds.

We had two near misses with the police while out on the vegetable round. Turning up a private drive, we were followed by a police car; the driver said we had a loose wire hanging out at the back of the van doors. It was connected to something inside the van, so that was no problem. But then he wanted to test the handbrake – which Philip knew was not very efficient. Fortunately he had the wit to engage reverse gear so when the police officer tried to push the van forward, it remained immoveable!

The other occasion was when I was in the main street delivering an order. Our local garage owner crossed over the road and warned me that the Traffic Inspector who had condemned Leonard not long before was in the village and had spotted our van. He had gone to the garage and asked Bob if he knew the owner. He said the front wheels were 'pigeon-toed'. Bob, of course, said he had no idea at all who the van belonged to and having made sure the Inspector had driven out of sight, he rushed over the road to warn me. I took the van down to the service area and had the fault corrected.

To help us run the farm in summer we employed harvest campers from the establishment up the road at Kenardington. It was run by Reginald and Dorothy Parry who became good friends of ours. The campers were holiday makers who wanted an outdoor holiday, earning some pocket money at the same time. In the morning I would telephone the camp and specify the number of campers required – usually two, three or four and a lorry would later deposit them on the farm. The going rate of pay was one shilling and twopence an hour – around 7p. Some workers were worth more and others nothing at all. As, for example, the two pretty blonde girls set to pull up the weeds growing among the poled runner beans. A check on their work a few minutes after they had started revealed they were pulling up the beans and leaving the weeds! Some were real townsfolk, never before in the country . . . Giving them a hoe resulted in crops of enormous blisters on their hands. They were useful, on the whole, helping with haymaking and corn harvest and picking the apple crop.

I also supplied the vegetables and fruit to the camp. Mrs Parry telephoned the farm early in the day and when I found the time I delivered it to the camp. Sometimes I forgot; there would be a frosty telephone call and a thundercloud waiting for me outside the cookhouse. It darkened the air for some minutes until at last it would shout: "Oh for God's sake have a cup of coffee!!".

Reginald Parry was a large genial man with a good corporation on him – a cockney camper, arriving at the camp, viewed him and called out: "Bet that took some beer, Guv'nor!". At the time we had my father's partner at Queen Anne Street and his Canadian wife for the weekend: Elizabeth was expecting twins – which arrived soon afterwards. On my next visit to the camp I had toddler Nigel with me – usual known as 'Bubba Nigel', his first encounter with Mr. Parry. Nigel looked him up and down silently and then asked: "Are you having twins too, Mr. Parry?" There was a moment of stunned silence followed by a fierce bellow of laughter – thank goodness.

We had an orchard of two and a half acres and various cherry plums, morello cherries and damsons dotted around the farm. In our first two years we put the 'standing fruit' up for auction which meant wholesale pickers walked round the orchard sizing up the crop and offered a price. They were responsible for the picking and marketing of the fruit, providing their own equipment. It started around August Bank Holiday with the Gladstone and Beauty of Bath through Millers Seedling, Worcester Pearmain to the cookers, Lord Derby, King Edward VII, Bramley and an enormous apple with crimson/purple skins described as Hoary Morn. We offered the orchard for auction only in 1947 and 1948 [it made £200 each sale] because the markets then started accepting foreign produce which had not been in the country for some years, due to the war and the home markets had a monopoly. Much of the trouble stemmed from the fact that our produce came on the market at the same time as every other market gardeners'. The only way to obtain a better return was to invest in glasshouses. I had neither the experience nor the capital for this but Philip went off to Swanley for a year, learning the glasshouse trade. Audrey and I would have been happy to have called it a day but we had the five year lease to complete. I was able to borrow capital from my mother's family legal firm and we ordered a 70 x 40 feet Dutch light greenhouse and Philip, armed with his new knowledge, came back to run it.

The farm lived up to its usual tricks and the greenhouse and its erection team arrived from the north of England at midnight in a blinding snowstorm. They dossed down on the sitting room floor for the night. I also bought an Allen Motor Scythe plus a hedge trimmer and an orchard sprayer working from the machine. The Allen Scythe later proved the backbone of my churchyard cutting service.

The greenhouse proved successful and Philip grew some excellent crops of early lettuce – their quality was such that our Hastings wholesaler rang up to order a consignment for a lunch at which Princess Elizabeth was to be present. Tomatoes followed next and finally late flowering chrysanthemums, standing outside all the summer and taken in when the tomatoes were cleared. Had we been able to adopt this aspect of farming it might have been a different matter. The best offer received at the fruit auction in 1949 was only thirty pounds and we decided to pick and market the fruit ourselves. We never attempted to cost the profits and I rather doubt if there would have been any. We had the rent, rates, cost of pruning the orchard, mowing the grass, spraying the crop and our labour for picking the crop, cost of wholesaler transport to markets and the commission.

It was the same with the market garden produce. Early crops made reasonable prices. During the war anything remotely resembling a vegetable made a decent price. Once the early produce had been sent off, gluts tended to appear. Once we sent off half a ton of runner beans and not one was sold in Covent Garden yet we had to pay the rail charge and the cost of picking the beans.

At the beginning of 1952 it was obvious the farm would never pay its way and the landlord's lawyer wrote to tell us that he wished to sell the farm and offered us first refusal – but at a quite unrealistic price. We could not agree on a figure nor could we afford to carry on renting and losing five hundred pounds annually. After protracted negotiations we resigned the tenancy without either party paying compensation. We gave up the farm after six years of unremitting and unrewarding hard work. It had been a mistake from the start, given the conditions then and later. Too scattered for one thing and too large for one man to manage on his own, yet not big enough for two – the glasshouses solution was probably best, giving up the scattered fields and concentrating on the homestead – about five acres.

Two last examples of the bad luck that dogged us. A few weeks after our new greenhouse had been erected, I returned from playing the organ on Easter Sunday to find some of the Dutch lights in the greenhouse had been broken and lying dead nearby were two partridges. It seemed they were French partridges because they had red noses. I applied to the insurance company for compensation and was told that we were not covered – this is hardly a new story, of course. The policy covered us for almost every sort of disaster, from fire raising maniacs, flood, tempest, atomic warfare . . . but damage caused by partridges (French or otherwise) – no.

A splendid example of Things Going Wrong was demonstrated by the chimney fire. A normal house might have a fire developing in the chimney which resulted in a lot of smoke and sparks flying out of the top of the stack – and that was that. But our chimney pot actually exploded – not once but several times over a period of half an hour. Every few minutes we heard another sharp crackling and further pieces of chimney pot came crashing to the ground . . . Kind neighbours called round to inform us that our chimney was on fire – and stayed to watch the pyrotechnics. Finally there was one last colossal explosion and the remnants of the earthenware pot took off vertically and landed in the back garden.

Earlier readers will remember how our new vicar suggested the churchyard maintenance service; how I started by sending out ninety copies of a circular letter to the clergy within a thirty mile radius and how they met with an immediate and successful response the very next morning. We stayed with my parents for a year at Bench Hill, outside Woodchurch and Easter 1954 returned to Appledore for a further year before moving to Biddenden. We rented half of a 16th century cottage from a friend in the village. I carried on as Appledore organist until Easter 1955.

In Biddenden we lived in the council estate known as Chulkhurst, named after the famous Biddenham Siamese twins Eliza and Mary Chulkhurst. We lived in number 54 from Easter 1955 to February 1958 and after we gave up our tenancy the house was subsequently the scene of a family tragedy. An unemployed father of five children cut the throats of his wife and five children as they lay asleep one night and then tried to hang himself in the electric sub-station nearby. He succeeded only in nearly burning off one arm and subsequently spent a term of imprisonment in a mental institution. I often considered we were lucky to be spared the ordeal of a pre-ordained haunting where an event in the future 'casts its shadows before'. I was told by my former friends in the houses nearby that no one heard a sound during the night and the first they knew of the tragedy was when the police arrived to investigate.

CHAPTER EIGHT

Organs

This organ playing business has cropped up from time to time and a lot of people have asked how I became involved in the organ world. As related, it began when my father took me with him to Uxbridge and I had the run of the harmoniums and American organs in Willis' music shop. After our move to Mill End Mr. Willis kindly allowed me to buy a second hand American organ for half price – this was the organ which I used to play in my outside room. My prep. school stood next to All Saints Church, Gerrards Cross and the organist came along one morning to find some boys for his choir. He scraped the bottom of the barrel and included me one week but I was in the choir for only one Sunday and turfed out by the next. I was fascinated by the sight of the organist disappearing through a little door in the wall and appearing high above my head in the organ loft.

How did the transition from my little organ to a church organ take place? I was cycling through the hamlet of West Hythe, a short distance towards Uxbridge and stopped to look in the church. There I spied an excellent organ with two manuals and pedals. It was not locked so I opened the console, went round to the back and pumped the bellows full of air, then rushed round to play some chords until the wind supply gave out with a hollow gasp. I soon discovered that a single quiet stop lasted much longer than a blast on the full organ. Badly smitten, I made inquiries about Permission to practise; the organist was a delightful old gentleman who resembled a saint in a stained glass window and he obtained permission for me to play as much as I liked for a fee of ten shillings a quarter. From Merchant Taylors it was a twelve mile round journey to the organ and the friends I persuaded to accompany me and act as blowers showed a distressing desire to try the organ themselves and let me do the blowing.

In 1937 the Vicar of Rickmansworth kindly allowed me to play the parish church organ for a shilling an hour and he hoped I gained as much pleasure from it as he had done as a boy. This was a two manual organ with the lowest keyboard, the choir organ 'prepared for'. This meant the keys were solid, not connected to anything and dropping the hands on it could result in a strained finger. The noteworthy thing I accomplished here was to jam the key in the glass fronted doors and no one managed to retrieve it; still stuck in the lock when I left Rickmansworth late in 1940. I tried the experiment once of removing the bottom trumpet pipe and taking it home where I connected it up to the household Hoover working in reverse and producing a splendid racket, even without the tube part, which of course I had to leave in the swell box being about eight feet long.

We had a fine modern three manual Willis in the Great Hall at Merchant Taylors but as I did not take piano lessons I could not gain permission to play it. Baulked in my efforts to play and having a friend in the school choir who unlocked the organ every morning for Mr. Waller, the organist, I persuaded him to take an impression of the yale key in plasticene. I bought a matching blank key in Watford Woolworth and handed the impression and the key blank to the Manor gardener; later he presented me with the key, which I soon tried in the console lock, overjoyed to find it turned, released the roll top and the organ was open before me! I played a few soft chords, showered all my available wealth on the gardener – amounting, I believe, to a shilling and ninepence.

It was absurd really, without permission I could never hope to play the organ other than surreptitiously, terrified by the thought of being found out. My friend and fellow organ fanatic Herbert Hackett insisted on trying his hand but the first thing he did was to pull out the sixteen foot Trombone pedal stop and press down bottom E flat! A tremendous rumble reverberated round the Great Hall and ten seconds later we had vanished . . . I shot up to the Manor to establish some sort of an alibi.

Another church organ with which I became involved was in the parish church, Watford. This possessed a splendid three manual organ with the console in the south chancel aisle and the pipework away in the north transept. Getting it open was a problem but after several visits I located the key, artfully hidden away from anyone but a fanatic like myself. I then asked if I might practise out of school hours and the answer came back – certainly, at a fee of ten shillings an hour. This seemed excessive, Rickmansworth being only a shilling an hour, although of course it was a much bigger organ. My pocket money amounted to a regular shilling and sixpence weekly, so I was not in a financial condition to accept the offer. I used to pedal over to Watford and play for a few minutes when ever opportunity offered. Herbert was with me once and we were appalled to see two gentleman coming towards us . . . "What do you think, shall we finish with hymn 24?" I asked him and started playing it over. The gentlemen nodded and smiled as they moved away. We wiped the perspiration from our brows!

This business of the organ key inspired me to set about making a master key for the school doors – I knew the janitor had such a key since I had seen him using it. By careful and artful observation I calculated how to make a master key and was able to open any locked door that I wished. I took the choirboy who had supplied the organ key impression on a tour of the school one Sunday morning, unfortunately one of the prefects was taking his parents on a tour and he saw us coming out of a room which he knew was kept locked and he reported it to our deputy house master, a very decent man, F.K. Paul who had been my Lower Fourth A form master, both of us being new that September 1933.

Well, of course the next item on my agenda was a polite request to pop along to Paul's study and explain about the master key, he had also heard vague rumours of the organ playing and he demanded an explanation of my activities. He heard me through and said it would go no further. . . A day or two later the housemaster DD asked to see me and he also wanted to hear my story – I was word perfect by that time – and he also said it would go no further. Two days later during morning lessons came a summons to have a little chat with the headmaster, N.P. Birley. He also heard me out in silence and pointed out that R.B. had made a master key, gone into the secretary's office and stolen forty concert tickets . . . and he had been turfed out.

I pointed out that I had made the key for the fun of it not for thieving purposes and the interview terminated quite amicably.

So of course the future looked pretty bleak. All right, perhaps, to escape of my own free will but to be thrown out was not in the scheme devised for me by my parents. In fact the authorities were very lenient. I was not allowed to practise in Rickmansworth for the rest of that term only and I had to send Watford church a calculated practising fee based on the time I reckoned I had played there. Nothing more was said; I daresay they had a conference and had decided that a deaf eccentric had better not be pushed too far or he might go clean over the edge. I was thankful to get off so lightly and also even more profoundly relieved that the headmaster had not still been Spencer Leeson; I would never have survived any sort of an interview with him. Looking back, I was clearly trusted to keep to the agreement not to play in Rickmansworth church for the next few weeks and give a fair calculation of my times on the Watford organ

After moving to Aylesbury as a farm pupil in October 1940 I lodged in the farm house with Richard Rowland and his wife. She kindly gained me permission to play the organ at Holy Trinity in Walton Street and furthermore she contacted the vicar of the parish church and I was able to play there – four years later Audrey and I were married there.

I remember one amusing incident at Holy Trinity during a harvest festival evensong which Audrey and I attended. The church was filling rapidly and the gallery was brought into use. The verger walked backward down the passage, conducting two late entrants to a bottom tier seat and his back nudged a plant balanced on the ledge. Audrey and I were watching and saw the plant sail through the air and land unerringly on the head of a lady praying directly in its downward path. By a miracle she was unhurt, the pot had turned upside down during its journey and landed leafy plant side on her hat.

The best of the Aylesbury organs was in St John's church and it was in a gallery high above the chancel. The organist was supposed to leave the organ door unlocked for me but he rarely remembered to do so. I had to swarm up the wall behind the choir stalls and gain access to the organ gallery by climbing over the railing, an athletic feat that left me panting and breathless. The lower door had a yale lock so I had only to walk down the staircase behind the organ, open the door and pull it shut behind me. It was a fine organ and I spent many happy hours playing it. My climbing performance reminded me of Dracula and given a cloak, a shovel hat, a pair of red eyes and sharp canine teeth, I could have impersonated him to the life.

I obtained this organ through the good offices of Audrey and her brother; the latter had been in the choir in his younger days and the Vicar, Revd Eric Pearson, married us in the parish church in April 1944. He held a private communion service for the pair of us on our wedding day, despite the tradition that decreed bride and groom should not meet on the wedding day before the service itself.

To hearken back to Merchant Taylors. My fellow enthusiast Herbert had a younger brother Peter, who was in the Temple Church choir; the organist and choirmaster was the world famous Dr. George Thalben-Ball. A contemporary of Peter's was Ernest Lough, who had made a best selling record of Mendlesson's O For the Wings of a Dove. Herbert and I went to a Sunday service at the Temple church and Peter introduced us to Dr. Thalben-Ball who kindly took us into the organ loft and demonstrated the organ and then invited us to accompany him into the organ loft for choral evensong. This would have been a memorable event for us seventeen year olds but unfortunately Sir Walford Davies turned up and went into the organ loft instead. I daresay, as Master of the King's Music, he had a better right than we had.

The Temple church services were the most beautifully sung and exciting services I have ever attended. One minute the choir would be almost whispering, the organ accompanying on a soft flute. Then all of a sudden the choir would blaze into life, louder and louder . . . more stops being added on the organ and then a terrific climax, the choir in full cry and the organ crashing in with a tremendous last chord bringing in full organ dominated by the powerful thirty-two foot pedal reed.

I was allowed to play the organ in the Middlesex hospital; the organ was in a gallery at the back of the chapel, a lovely little building which seemed to be placed with the wards all round it. Matron roped me in to play for a service so I went along with Herbert and all went well until the third hymn. I played over the tune in front of me and my first chords were followed by a silence – which tells an organist that Something Has Gone Wrong. Sure enough, there was a patter of feet and Matron rushed in, ripped away my hymn book and substituted another. Fortunately I was able to sight-read the music and in their relief at having a tune they recognised the congregation fairly raised the roof. Afterwards I started Handel's Largo and after a few chords I slid off the end of the organ stool on the bass side while Herbert moved along from the treble and took over the music without a break – a veritable triumph of co-ordination.

Former readers will recall how I became Organist of Appledore parish church after Easter 1948 where my deafness really did prove a handicap and I mentioned some of the misfortunes I suffered but a few more might cause some amusement. I tended to play the next chant before the lesson had ended and brought in Amens before the end of prayers. I did this when we had a visiting lay reader and shot off an Amen halfway through one of his prayers. I apologised profusely after the service and he charmingly said I need not worry at all, he thought the Amen in the middle of the prayer added an extra dimension.

One painful morning I gave out the chant for the psalm, looked in my little driving mirror and was astounded to see the Vicar conferring with Mrs Mac., our leading choirlady. The Vicar came across the chancel and told me that Mrs Mac. had said it was the wrong chant. "Rubbish," I told him "Of course it's the right chant. I'll play it again". Which I did, looked in the mirror and there they were, deep in a confabulation! The Vicar toddled over again! "Mrs Mac. says IT IS THE WRONG CHANT". Once again I checked my service sheet, told him it was the right chant and would play it for a third time. This led to Mrs Mac. herself coming over and after a brief argument I gave way and played over the evening chant instead; it seem to be the only way of getting on with the service. I received a handsome apology after the service as in fact I had been right and she had been wrong.

At the end of my second or third service I was ready to play a lusty Amen after the blessing and as the Vicar held up his hand to deliver it he suddenly gave a hollow groan and collapsed on the altar steps. Disaster! A bevy of ladies rushed to pick him up and carry him into the vestry behind the organ and from around the corner came a prodigious aroma of brandy. I always maintained that it came from a bottle carried by Mrs Ticehurst in her hip pocket although she denied this. Quite recently, forty-three years later I asked one of her daughters and she said her mother had the brandy bottle in her capacious handbag.

After I had been organist for a year Mrs Ticehurst brought the Church Council's attention to the fact I had received no payment whatever for my exertions and Something Should Be Done. I was awarded a salary of twenty-six pounds annually and an immediate cheque for five pounds. With the cheque I bought a chiming clock which went for a year and then stopped. Not even its maker could restore it to further life and I used some of the parts to mend the farm tractor. The salary was paid quarterly save once when I had a terrific row with the church treasurer and he withheld it for six weeks.

Philip joined the choir as a tenor but when things went wrong he took care to take no part in the proceedings, simply looking up at the church roof until the whites of his eyes showed. It was left to one of the other men to turn round and give my cassock a sharp tug when disaster had struck again.

By the autumn of 1951 I was feeling pretty uppish and while I realised I could never give an organ recital I reckoned that if I took Thalben-Ball's place in the Temple church hardly anyone would notice the difference. At this time I made the acquaintance of Gerald Knight, the organist of Canterbury cathedral. In response to my timid letter he kindly invited me to tea at his house in The Precincts and afterwards to accompany him to the organ loft for choral evensong. This was a wonderful experience and the lessons I absorbed from watching and listening to a cathedral organist transformed my ideas of church musicianship. Gerald became a friend of the family and almost godfather to Charmian and on a number of occasions Audrey and Philip came with me in the organ loft. (He said he had too many godchildren).

In 1952 Gerald offered to give a recital in Appledore church in aid of church funds and he brought with him a tenor from the cathedral choir to sing solo pieces. They arrived at six o'clock and we took them round the farm, ending up in our new greenhouse containing some hundreds of tomato plants. At twenty-five past six Gerald suggested that perhaps we had better stroll along to the church and we arrived at the vestry door with two minutes to spare! The Vicar and choir were in a pitiable state of panic. No one could blame them since not only had the famous cathedral organist failed to appear but their own highly inferior product had also vanished – leaving them with a packed congregation who might turn uncommonly ugly when told there was no organist of any sort . . .

Gerald just about stood my nine stop organ on one corner. The solo tenor asked one of our choir members if he could have a glass of water and Monty Bates (he was our butcher and a churchwarden) hurried over the churchyard to the Red Lion and banged on the back door. When it was opened it was nearly slammed in his face. It seemed that the landlady thought the surplice was a shroud and one of the churchyard inmates had climbed out for a quick one, having worked up a thirst over the centuries.

Mention of ghosts brings me to another experience which I hope will amuse the reader. In 1953 we were expecting a new Vicar and Archbishop Fisher said that he would come and take the service of

Institution and Induction with the Archdeacon of Maidstone, Julian Bickersteth. I think this came about because after the departure of the Reverend Alfred Mayne we were without a vicar for eighteen months and much of the trouble was that Fisher would not appoint the man we wanted. We had heated arguments at church meetings, letters floated back and forth between Appledore and Canterbury and finally Archdeacon Bickersteth came to take a service and pour oil on troubled waters. He told us we could forget about the man from Norfolk. If he was positively the last clergyman left in the whole country, the Archbishop had not the slightest intention of posting him to Appledore. For one thing, he was too high church and he then appointed a man who was even higher church and told him to keep it low!

The news that the archbishop was coming in person put me in a state of mortal panic. I decided to learn Bach's Toccata and Fugue in D minor and purchased the music. It was quickly apparent that getting to grips with the Toccata was going to absorb all my energies without including the Fugue as well. It entailed an immense amount of practising, often in the church after the day's work was done. The result of all this frenzied activity was to raise a pair of ghosts.

At first I was aware of 'someone' standing behind the organ stool staring at me; this just made me feel uncomfortable. I could see nobody and I gained a feeling of dislike. This was the first time I had come up against the supernatural – it was not to be my last.

One chilly night I was playing away, just the chancel lights on behind me and I became aware of a short brown cowled shape on my right by the end of the choir stall. The immediate reaction was to rise six inches off the organ stool and come to rest, a solid mass of nerves. The shape turned out to be my old brown overcoat hanging over the choir stall but my nerve was broken and I hurried home.

An old family friend was a professional medium and I explained this creepy business to her; on her next visit she came along to hold a seance in the church. With us came my father and our young vicar. Both were profound sceptics – the Vicar apparently not believing in angels and he certainly did not believe Mrs Snowden when she asserted she could see the church's guardian angel.

She asked me to play the organ and stopped me after ten minutes saying she had discovered the cause of my problem. She said she had seen two old people rise out of the chancel floor, dressed in clothing of about the fourteenth century. They told her that they understood that after they died they would sleep until the Last Trump sounded, when they must rise up, put on clean shrouds and face the Judgement. Well, they heard the Last Trump sounding but unfortunately it had been a false alarm, being the organist beating up Bach's Toccata in D minor. Thereafter they were unable to regain their previous slumbers and hovered around the chancel whenever the deep tones of the organ sounded. Mrs Snowden explained their beliefs were at fault and told them to move on to their full spiritual life and take no notice of the organ. I fear they refused to listen to her and were still on the prowl when I left the church in 1955. My psychic sense had developed further by then and I was able to see them from the corner of my eye, moving around the nave of the church. I tried testing car headlights coming along the road from the Marsh below the church to see if shadows were cast similar to what I saw but this was never the case.

Ten years later I met the current organist of Appledore church who told me she would never practise at night because of a strong feeling of being watched.

After we left Appledore I did not have a regular organ job but deputised when needed, first in Biddenden, then Hythe, Cheriton and finally my present church for over twenty years, Newington, outside Folkestone, site of the Channel Tunnel work

The Toccata in D minor is an organist's show piece and having learnt it I played it on every organ I came across, from the Royal Albert Hall to Canterbury cathedral – and a good many in between, as Gerald Knight had proposed me as a member of the Kent Organists' Association and we met in churches all over the county. One of these was Tonbridge School chapel, which possessed a fine organ up in a gallery. Philip was with me; following my usual custom I went up with other members into the organ loft to try the organ and – of course! – played the Toccata. Philip was listening down below, two members were standing next to him and one said to the other:"My God, THERE HE GOES AGAIN!!" Philip gleefully reported this to me when I came down and it killed stone dead any further performances.

On a visit to my uncle and aunt in Odcombe near Yeovil I was pressed into playing for both Sunday services. In the morning the choir were thrown into a panic by having a proper organist playing for them and they started singing at top speed. I simply could not keep up with them and my playing of the Te Deum went something like this: We praise Thee O God, we . . . Thee . . . Lord. All . . . earth . . . Thee . . . Father . . . lasting. I don't suppose the Te Deum had been sung so fast since it was introduced by Cranmer at the Reformation.

Before evensong I begged the choir with tears in my eyes not to sing so quickly. It was certainly better but unfortunately my collar had come off its stud and it took a time to put it back. My aunt told me after the service that one of the choirgirls had been fascinated by me and I pointed out she had probably never seen an organist who wore his collar just below his nose.

The last time I played in Odcombe was for my uncle's funeral in a very cold February. After practising for half an hour I came out as stiff as a plank. I had a two-page piece with which to play in my uncle, I came to the end, no sign of him. I played it again, played it upside down, sideways and possibly backwards by which time I was at the end of my tether when thank goodness the church door flew open and my uncle's coffin came down the nave. Another minute and I would have left the organ and fetched him in myself.

Gerald Knight was a perfectionist and he never entertained any notions about farmer Jack laying his hands on his cathedral organ. "Be ye musically perfect even as your Father in heaven is musically perfect" was never a doctrine to which I subscribed. I had the temerity to play Chopin's Nocturne in E flat [opus 9 No.2] when Gerald was present for tea. Afterwards he commented quite kindly that if one could not play a piece of music perfectly it was better not to attempt it at all. He applied this standard to church choirs. If a choir could not sing the service really well it was better to say everything. By my reckoning this would silence three quarters of the choirs in the United Kingdom and Eire! Surely it is better for the local musicians to do their best? The results may not be pleasing to a highly trained musical ear but that is not to say it is unacceptable to Almighty God.

Allan Wicks became the cathedral organist in the early 1960's and he took a more tolerant view. I met him in Goudhurst while I was cutting the churchyard and he was practising the organ for a recital given later that evening. He cheerfully suggested I tried the cathedral organ – great fun, he added. By then Old Miss Hunter had left me two hundred pounds as a legacy and I spent some on a tape recorder. I made an appointment with Allan to go in the organ loft with him for evensong and play the organ afterwards. My family were busy in the week and my radiogram organ recitals often met with complaints. "How long is it going on for?" and "Do you HAVE to play it so loudly?" I asked an Indian friend to come with me and work the recorder. So Beryl and I had tea in Canterbury first and then went up into the loft with Allan. Evensong ended, he played his concluding voluntary, turned to me and said: "It's all yours!".

One by one the lights were turned out until the cathedral was in complete darkness with just the light over the console illuminating the organ loft.

It might have been very romantic, alone in the cathedral with a beautiful Indian lady but my thoughts were entirely on the organ and the hour in front of me to play anything I liked. I started with a simple Bach Prelude and no power-hungry organist will be surprised to learn that as I neared the end of the piece, my hand shot out and added the Contra Posaune, a metal reed stop of enormous power and profundity and I used the bottom C . . . A tremendous volume of sound poured down from the triforium, beat furiously round our heads and heaved itself off into the far corners of the cathedral. It was a supreme moment of magic. Perhaps not a very good tape recording but after twenty-seven years I can still play it and regain something of that thrilling hour.

Later in the summer I played it again, my bank manager churchyarding friend John came with me. Allan handed us the cathedral key and went off to Oxford. Then I spent an afternoon in the cathedral photographing the organ pipes. Contrary to what many people seem to think, the pipes are not in the organ loft but high up in the south triforium. To gain access I had to climb a spiral staircase in the south east transept and walk through a low doorway on to a passage about fifty feet above the floor, maybe a yard wide and nothing to stop me from stepping off the edge and landing on the floor far below. Hating heights, I sidled along the passage way, my back pressed against the wall. Once inside the triforium itself the area was so large I no longer felt any vertigo and I took some excellent photographs which later were used in Kent Life.

I was highly amused when an officious cathedral gentleman in a bowler hat toiled all the way up the staircase to ask me what I was doing there and letting off a flash gun every few minutes. With quiet dignity I told him I had permission from Allan and he had perforce to turn round and make his way down again!

Our new vicar in 1953 also ran Kenardington parish a few miles away and Archdeacon Bickersteth conducted a service to install him into the living. The church possessed a harmoniumin near the chancel – a good one with twenty stops which included a 'growler', a heavy reed stop which went down to F below normal bottom C. When used in the right manner this stop sounded like some prehistoric monster roaring after its prey. The archdeacon came in behind the clergy and the congregation began on the first hymn – Rejoice the Lord is King, bellowing it out in fine style. Until it came to the last verse which was over the page, something I had not realised. The people took a collective deep breath, ready to render this verse as it had seldom been rendered before. What happened? The harmonium remained silent and the organist was blowing his nose . . . There was a hissing of air let out of over-inflated lungs.

In spite of this mishap, after the service was over and my final blast on the prehistoric monster had died away, Archdeacon Bickersteth came rushing down the nave, hand outstretched. "Mr Jack," he said heartily, "I have never heard a harmonium played like that before!". Probably not, having never encountered an organist with such an unscrupulous musical ability.

For example, when our organist, Fred Skinner, in Hythe parish church offered me organ lessons in return for hedge cutting, I gave it up after ten minutes. "Hoi!", said Fred. "Where's that tied note?" I explained, ha ha, I never bothered about tied notes. "You are going to worry about this one, chum", was his rejoinder and I realised he and I were musically poles apart.

As I said earlier, we were without a vicar in Appledore for eighteen months and various clergy came along to take services. Two of them were extremely old gentlemen. one had been a vicar of Appledore about a hundred years earlier and his voice production was so feeble I hardly heard a word he said. He took so long quavering out his intoned responses that I thought he had finished by the time he had reached the half way mark and therefore pitched in with the organ response and cut him off.

The other old parson considered himself to be such a remarkable preacher that he made the choir move down to the nave during the last verse of the pre-sermon hymn so that they could the more easily catch his words of wisdom. Afterwards they processed back to the choirstalls singing the last hymn. I did not approve of this at all. Our singing was hardly robust at the best of times without the extra hazard of the choir negotiating the chancel steps as well. So one Sunday when Canon S. was absent, I told the choir to stay in their choir stalls during the sermon. Canon S. heard about this defiance of his wishes the following Sunday. Directly after the service had ended he hurried across to the organ from the sanctuary ("hot from the blessing" as I described it later), and we started a furious row, joined by the choirmaster. It ended with the choirmaster resigning and Canon S. storming off in a fury.

A most bizarre event took place when the Vicar's old dog came into the church. It was not the first time – I related earlier how Mr. Mayne had started the Lord's Prayer and found he had been joined by the Vicarage pet. "Our father, which art in heaven (down Druid!) Hallowed be Thy name (Druid, will you go away!)" and so on. This time Druid wandered into the chancel and the churchwarden Mr. Colthup decided to take a hand and eject him. He chased him round the chancel and into the vestry but Druid went back again by the sanctuary door, followed by a furious churchwarden. They rushed twice round the sanctuary and the altar before Druid was finally captured and led away in disgrace.

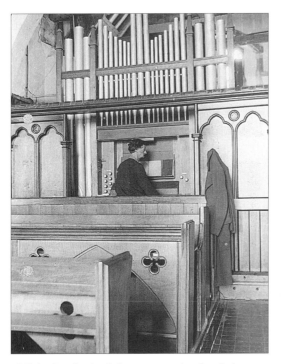

Michael at the Appledore organ – the ghastly brown coat hanging over the choir stalls.

A wonderful view from the inside of the great organ at Canterbury Cathedral of the 32' Contraposaune.

Michael enjoying himself on the Canterbury Cathedral organ – perhaps about to pull out the Contraposaune.

CHAPTER NINE

A Holt Eccentric

Former readers may recall my great aunt Alexandra and her funeral. Her brother Alexander was another larger than life Victorian eccentric. He died before the last war of senile decay, aggravated by Frustrated Poaditis and his active years coincided with the golden years of Victorian church attendance. He really retired after his beloved organ was blown up during the first World War.

I must say something about the 'Poaditis' mentioned above. The latin name for organist is pulsator organorum – literally 'beater of organs' which in those far off days is what the performer did quite literally. Organists as a class are consumed with a desire to play every organ on which they can lay their hands – perhaps not so much cinema organs, although I have felt the urge and spent a happy hour playing on the organ in the Odeon, Leicester Square years ago. The merest thought, let alone the viewing of an organ console (the larger the better) causes the organist's fingers to begin an intolerable twitching and so we have 'organist's twitching fingers' translated back into latin as Pulsator Organorum Agitans Digitorum or POAD for short. My uncle Alexander was a fine example of a full blown Poad, a state which could be termed 'Poaditis' and therefore when he was no longer able to get about due to increasing infirmity, it became Frustrated Poaditis – which could easily have been fatal in a younger man, let alone in an old nuisance of ninety.

Alexander was for many years the organist and choirmaster of a fashionable Sydenham church and he maintained a large choir of men and boys, despite his eccentric behaviour. First, the choir were well paid, the men receiving ten shillings and the boys two shillings for each completed Mattins, evensong and choir practice. For boys the waiting list was so astronomical that parents put down their sons for the choir as soon as the sex of the new arrival had been determined. This was in Victorian and Edwardian days when money was worth much more.

There were times when the better singers were tempted to move to another church, losing patience with their choirmaster and his choral ideas. Alexander would never accept a resignation, seizing the offender by the elbow and walking him up and down the church until he gave in. It would be pointed out that no one else could pay his rates, that the church was always packed on Sunday and it was necessary to give the congregation what it wanted – after the fashion of some modern churches which jazz up the liturgy to attract a larger attendance.

Nowadays choirmasters must treat their choir members with velvet gloves; they are hard to replace and appallingly sensitive to criticism. Alexander was able to bawl out anybody who failed to come up to scratch. An archdeacon friend of the vicar's once attended choir practice and said afterwards in his usual patronising way: "Not a bad choir you've got there, Mr. Holt." My uncle glared at him in disgust and retorted that the speaker might be an archdeacon (in a tone of voice which suggested someone had slipped up over the appointment) but he, Alexander Holt, would go down on his knees that night and thank God the archdeacon was not a choir member. The wretched fellow could only manage a weak titter as Alexander strode off.

He possessed a strong sense of reverence and when his organ blower – a friend of many years' standing – so far forgot himself as to fry up a couple of Yarmouth bloaters on an oil stove in the vestry, he found himself sacked on the spot.

When Alexander took over as organist he had only a small organ to play but shortly after his appointment he was fortunate enough to hear of a Pfeife and Bagwasche organ going cheaply. He persuaded the church authorities to buy it and he undertook the installation of the organ himself. On the whole he was pretty successful. Occasionally the organ gave a loud scream for no apparent reason or it might give a thin wail which put the vicar's wife in mind of a starving baby. The crowning glory of the organ was the pedal reed – a sixteen foot trombone. This was a 'real whopper' and one of Bagwasche's finest efforts. It once rumbled away so splendidly that St John the Baptist fell clean out of his window.

I must confess that my uncle was not a very good musician but he possessed an instinct for musical showmanship. Never a noisy player, he knew when to finish with a strong climax. At the end of an anthem with the choir on the ultimate fortissimo chord and almost full organ, my uncle would pull out the Trombone. A terrific surge of sound rolled round the church and people sank back in their pews murmuring "Glorious, O utterly glorious!". Shades of Thalben-Ball at the Temple church years later. . .

Uncle's notable and eccentric genius showed in his handling of the anthems; the church performed one every other Sunday. The church was always packed to capacity when it was known that a big anthem was to be sung. You may ask why? Well, he would take an anthem and find some notes were too high for his tenors or trebles. He would therefore lower them until everyone was happy. This meant altering the other parts to accommodate the changed chords. Or there might be passages he found too difficult to play, so he juggled with those notes also. In the end the anthem by no means sounded exactly as the composer had intended and the huge congregations assembled to hear what the latest offering sounded like. Alexander's technique might have improved, in which case the anthem would be a more faithful rendering of the original or his technique might well have slipped a few cogs producing musical interest either way. There was one strict rule, the first and last bars were always played as written by the composer, even if the old boy had to sit up half the night learning them by heart.

The business of trebles and tenors singing their high notes was brilliantly solved by my artful uncle. The choir members were stood on hassocks of varying height. A tenor who could not reach top G would be stood on hassocks of increasing height until he could. A difficulty arose when a short fat boy could reach his notes easily while a tall thin boy needed a five inch hassock. The choir processed into church not according to their real heights but depending on the levels when standing on their hassocks.

A cathedral organist reprimanded Alexander for his inaccurate playing. He was obliged to admit he did not always play the printed notes . . . But then the choir knew his little ways and anyway the congregation never noticed any difference; it saved him a lot of trouble.

The opening organ recital on the newly-installed organ was given by the same cathedral organist. After the recital he had to retire to bed with the curtains drawn and resigned his appointment six weeks later, a broken man. The organ lasted until 1916 when a passing Zeppelin dropped a hand grenade down the vestry chimney and blew the whole caboodle to bits. The destruction of his beloved organ caused Uncle Alexander much anguish; he never again possessed the same driving force. Although he lingered on for a number of years he sank into a state of senile decay – aggravated, as I said, by Frustrated Poaditis. He spent many hours listening to gramophone organ records, his feet and fingers twitching away out of control.

The day arrived when he was in his final coma, the family gathered round his bed. Suddenly his eyes opened wide and a beatific smile spread across his face. "They say I can have a go!", he whispered and fell back dead on his pillow.

CHAPTER TEN

Dogs

Our first Appledore dog was an Australian Terrier named Peter but soon nicknamed Beetle. He met a sad early death chasing our local cop on his motor cycle and being run over. I went back to the breeder for a similar dog which we also called Beetle; he was with us for fourteen years and became a noted character. He was a tremendous hunter, anything was grist for his mill. We put it down to an early experience on the farm. Our storage building, the wartime fire station, was built on nissen hut lines with a circular roof composed of curved concrete sections covered with tarred felt and lined internally with a species of compressed cardboard. In consequence of the space between outer roof and inner skin rats and mice were able to take up residence and find a good living from the animal foodstuffs, grain, apples and market garden produce stored in the barn. Philip and I held regular hunts to keep down the rodent population and had already tried our cats, who failed miserably to do the job expected of them. Faced with a small army of the inmates advancing towards them, the cats simply turned tail and fled.

When Beetle was no longer a puppy we took him in with us on another ratting expedition. Inexperienced, he allowed a rat to bite his nose and from that moment his innate hunting instincts were aroused. He seized that rat by the neck and shook it, He threw it up in the air and caught it coming down. He smashed it against the floor until its bones cracked and thereafter, anything that moved was fair game to Beetle – rodents, rabbits, snakes, even butterflies were something to be hunted and killed. Audrey, Philip and I were raking up hay in one churchyard and Beetle was hunting around. He disappeared and a little later he turned up dragging a dead white rabbit behind him. We were perfectly aghast, popped the rabbit in a sack and departed the churchyard before any inquiries were made.

Beetle accompanied me daily on the churchyarding round but not always on the local lawn mowing. We lived in Hythe, my father had a dental practice in the High Street (having sold his Woodchurch house);

he and my mother lived in the flat over the practice. My mother used to spoil Beetle dreadfully, feeding him titbits of chicken and liver when ever we called there. He gained the idea of setting off from Albert Road and walking the ten minutes to my mother's kitchen, crossing busy (but then one way) Prospect Road to the High Street. Someone spotted him sitting on the edge of the pavement waiting for a gap in the traffic to enable him to cross the road. At my mother's he was regaled with a good meal – often eating cat Edward's dinner as well, and then trotted back to Albert Road. My mother suffered a severe heart attack in May 1960 and died three days later. Beetle never again went by himself to the flat although he came with us to see my father; also Audrey was acting as a receptionist in the surgery.

My mother had to bring him home once because he seemed to have pulled a muscle walking up the practice staircase. He looked very ill, eyes sunken, hot nose. We left him in front of the fire when we went to bed, fearing to find him dead in the morning. The pathetic little figure was still there; I lifted him gently and put him outside the garden gate. He was creeping along, barely able to lift his leg, when he spied a cat. Beetle hated cats and kept up an unrelenting war against them. Giving vent to a shrill bark, he set off down the road in pursuit of the enemy. Having seen it off, Beetle trotted jauntily back, all thought of illness forgotten. It must have been psychological..

While I was cutting my churchyards Beetle either went to sleep in the van or set off hunting; in remote country churchyards I could see him two fields away, nose down following some scent. Sometimes he had not returned when I was ready to leave: after clearing hay in Staple churchyard we had to leave without him and I asked the farmer opposite to look out for him. He came back of course, and spent the night on the daughter's bed. I had a forty-two mile round journey to collect him next day.

The Vicarage children in Goudhurst had guinea pigs and they gave a pair to our children but Beetle had them in the end. They escaped from their hutch one evening when we lived in Biddenden; Beetle went after them and they took refuge in a clump of brambles at the bottom of the garden. First he caught one and then around midnight Audrey heard a thin scream and Beetle came back to the house; when he was on the hunting trail he was deaf to all calls and threats. Later on the Goudhurst vicar showed me a fine guinea pig his children had just acquired. He opened the cage to take him out and SNAP! – Beetle had broken its neck in a second; I didn't know he had followed me to the Vicarage.

Beetle came to a sad end. He hunted once too often in the long grass and had a back leg almost severed by my mower. I rushed him to my Folkestone vet, who operated and put his leg in plaster. He returned home a few days later. I put him in his basket, picked up my lunch bag and prepared to leave. Beetle immediately struggled out of his basket and hobbled to the door, ready to go churchyarding. How could I leave him behind? A little later he developed Leukaemia (doubtless from the shock) and had to be put to sleep. but he spent his last days churchyarding. The healing in his leg caused him to nibble his paw; we could not stop him for he tore off any bandage we tied round it. I wrote to my spirit healer begging him to help and Beetle stopped nibbling his paw the next morning. Finally he had to be put to sleep; Audrey kindly took him as I could not face the ordeal. As a former vicedean of Canterbury cathedral said of him: "You were a grand dog and a gentleman".

To replace Beetle I acquired a Griffon – a breed I considered would look interesting sleeping on grave mounds. The first puppy was frightened of mowers, ran away from the tennis club in Hythe when I started up the Atco and was knocked down going home. To replace him we brought home Brabjoy Lorenzo, known as Nobby and he too spent the next fourteen years churchyarding with me.

But he was no hunter – couldn't even catch a mouse when it was placed in front of him and spent much of his time either sleeping in the van or sniffing among the gravestones. I thought this was very boring for him and suggested he took up reading some book. War and Peace was on television at the time and Nobby had the idea he would read the novel in the original Russian. I was obliged to point out to him I could not read Russian, knew nobody who could and why not try the Berry books by Dornford Yates since the Pleydell family possessed a dog called Nobby? So I gave him Berry and Co. to read and he enjoyed it. Mind you – he was a very slow reader and it took him a year to finish his first book. I had been explaining all this to a gentleman in Goudhurst cemetery and he asked me how Nobby turned over the pages? That was an easy one! "With his paws of course, same as you do". The gentleman nodded his head in agreement but I have really no idea if he believed me.

Again our pet's last days caused a lot of anguish. He developed cataracts on both eyes and he grew very deaf. Then he suffered a heart attack and our vet. judged it kinder to put him to sleep. A little before his death our seventeen year old cat had to be put to sleep and another vet. made such a horrible hash of the job that we decided not to endure such traumatic events again. Life is much simpler without pets.

My views on spiritualism lead me to believe that our loved pets survive death and carry on elsewhere as individuals in the care of someone who has gone before us, waiting for our arrival in the next sphere of living. It follows, therefore, that Beetle, still operating elsewhere, was able to transmit advice to his successor Nobby. From years of observing Nobby I was able to draw up a 'Code of Conduct' which Beetle might have sent Nobby as a guide to being a Churchyard Companion. This advice appeared in Dog's Life in June 1966 so I have re-written the article.

They tell me up here that you have taken over my role as a churchyard dog to my dear master. I am sure you will enjoy your life, travelling round the countryside, visiting different churchyards every day. But there are some things you should know The most important thing is to remain Top Dog and never let Master become too uppish – you are even smaller than me and therefore it is even more important to take a firm line with him.

For example, when he offers you a tit-bit from his lunch by no means always gulp it down greedily. First sniff at it carefully, as though you suspect it may be poisoned. Turn away and go to sleep, this usually annoys Master. Better still, give it a good lick before turning away in disgust. This will infuriate him as he cannot take it back and eat it himself. Of course if you have the chance, eat it later when he is not looking. That is, if you feel it is worth eating – this cannot always be relied on – I never did like his mixture of kipper, cheese and marmite in sandwiches.

In fact, never accept anything put down for you immediately – much better to approach any food with extreme caution. Give the impression you are afraid it may burn your tongue; try to suggest you fear it may explode in your face.

If you are shut in the van and Master has left his paper on the seat, scrabble it to pieces so that it becomes impossible for him to read it. Be careful to appear fast asleep on his return and convey the idea that you are never a dog that scrabbles paper. In similar vein, if you are given a piece of foam rubber to sleep on, scrabble an enormous hole right through the middle of it.

A good tip is to disappear just when master is finishing his churchyard and preparing to go home. At first he will just call you – remain out of sight. Presently he will become very cross and stamp about in the road . . . if you are lucky you might hear several interesting words. But be careful not to overdo it; he should be so relieved to see you trotting back that you will merely be lectured, thrown into the van and driven away.

You can make yourself a nuisance by chasing a cat up a tree and standing underneath, barking for hours – that annoys everybody within earshot! Even better is to inject a tortured yelping into your bark. People will come and tell Master that his poor little doggie is caught in a trap; the owner of the cat will come and tell him in no uncertain terms about monsters who allow their dogs to frighten poor little pussies. Either way Master will have to stop work and waste time talking.

Another well-tried plan is suddenly to bark furiously at nothing – pretend to see something invisible to Master. Introduce a note of fear into the bark. He is superstitious and will wonder if Someone Has Come Back. Do not overdo this act or he will suspect you are making a fool of him – or worse, that you are a fool yourself. Naturally this would never do!

In similar vein stand under a tree and look up into it, barking and whining. This will have everyone worried; they will go round and round the tree trying to spot your target. This again wastes Master's time.

If you are bored then find some mole runs and root them up. Master will then have to spend time filling them all in again. You should appear very keen and on the point of catching a mole, so you won't be punished although he will not be pleased.

You will have noted Master's tiresome habit of singing loudly and untunefully while driving the van, chiefly love songs and the psalms. Give a start and Stare at him with reproachful eyes until he abates the nuisance. You may, however, allow a certain level of singing without comment. On no account expect him to sing in tune; this he finds quite impossible!

The Young Masters in my day were easy to upset – almost anything would annoy them. They are older now but all the same, never be in a hurry to execute their orders. You must show you are fully aware of what they want – wag your tail or prick up your ears – but let them understand that a Top Dog is not prepared to accede to every request without consideration.

Another excellent tease is to bark suddenly about the time the postman is expected. Do this when Master is having breakfast by himself. As you know, he is deaf and will rush to the door to pick up the mail. Do not give too many false alarms; their frequency and effectiveness are in inverse proportion.

You must always be careful not to overdo the Master teasing or you will be classed as a nuisance and left at home. No amount of excited prancing and barking at the sight of the lunch bag being made ready will make the least bit of difference.

Above: *Beetle Dog in 1953 aged 14 months.*

Below: *Beetle Dog, although his leg had practically healed, died 7 days after this picture was taken.*

Above: *Nobby Griffon (1965).*

Below: *Nobby drinking from outside tap.*

The admonishing Thomas à Becket in Adisham churchyard. Nobby is sitting at the side of the platform to give an idea of the scale – in any case he loved being photographed.

CHAPTER ELEVEN

Churchyarding

Looking back across nearly forty years of churchyarding it is hard to pick out any highlights. A low light springs to mind at once – apart from the time Beetle nearly lost his leg. Nicholas and I were working on levelling and had replaced a grave slab; when I took my hand away the end of my middle finger was missing, cut off by the hard slate. The van was insured only for me to drive, therefore I had to drive home and attend our doctor's surgery. He telephoned the local casualty department in Folkestone to be told there was no one available to tackle that sort of job; I had to wait until the morning. Fortunately there was an able doctor on duty (although quite disagreeable) and he injected half a dozen pain killers into my finger, sliced off a piece of skin from my thigh and sewed it on top of my finger. I had asked for spirit healing the previous night and there was no pain at any time, even after the operation was over and the anaesthetic began to wear off there was no pain. Although I sensed that my finger was a raging fire it somehow did not register. The skin graft was successful and six weeks later the top joint was normal, if slightly lop sided. Nicholas was free at the time and did all my work; I learnt to use a grass hook left-handed and did what I could.

In my early days I had to estimate the cost of cutting each churchyard. The machine cutting of churchyards was then quite novel and I had no guides to help me. Originally I thought local farmers would be glad of the hay if it had been cut for them. Only a small handful of farmers ever did this and they were all churchwardens doing it from a sense of duty, sending in their men with hay rakes. It therefore fell to me to organise family parties on Saturdays to go out and clear those churchyards which had been mown the previous week. We also trimmed by hand those areas where the mower could not operate – mostly modern areas full of curbs and mounds.

We raked up the hay into large heaps and then set fire to them, which resulted in billowing clouds of smoke drifting round the area. The bonfires sometimes met with opposition from villagers and we had to point out that we were only doing the job because no one locally was willing to take it on.

In one churchyard we were visited by an elderly colonel who demanded in quavery tones that we dowsed our fires immediately. Meeting with a polite but firm refusal he went back to his womenfolk and was never seen again – probably executed for failing in his duty. One some Saturdays we might light as many as twenty-two bonfires!

In a remote and very overgrown place we lit half a dozen enormous fires and the smoke poured over the road into the cemetery opposite – a vast green hell of jungle quite beyond my mower. Several motorists were observed driving into the smoke but they never came out the other end. We presumed they had turned left into the cemetery and become lost. In that wilderness a car and its occupants could be lost for half a century and never discovered.

The worst trouble happened at Chilham. We were clearing the lower churchyard, had an excellent fire burning and a bearded frenzied figure came down the hill towards us, screaming imprecations. The church bells were driving him mad and our fire pushed him to the limit! He demanded we put out the fire at once . . . The smoke was driving up the hill into his house and doing hundreds of pounds' worth of damage to the contents – HUNDREDS of pounds, sir! He said I was no gentleman and not even a Christian. He ran a hosepipe down the hill and sprayed the fire until it was quiescent.

Nicholas and Nigel became experts at grass hooking, as did my bank manager friend John who liked nothing better than to come out churchyarding after a week in the bank. The rougher parts were cut either once a year or twice, if money was available. As I levelled the graves in most of my churchyards the amount of handwork declined.

The boys and I cleaned up an overgrown cemetery and on the way home I missed my sun glasses. We passed by the same place next day and called in to seek them. After a fruitless search I called off the boys and we drove away. Nicholas asked me what I thought a fair price would be for the recovery of the sun glasses.

Without stopping to think I said foolishly 'ten shillings'. Whereupon Nicholas produced them – hanging from the branch of a yew tree. A voice spoke from behind us: "And I want half a crown of that for keeping my mouth shut!".

My early days often meant round journeys of sixty miles daily. Some of them involved passing the old workhouse in Etchinghill outside Folkestone. (Its use for accommodating the 'Gentlemen of the Road' ended many years ago). In the early nineteen fifties any number of tramps set forth each morning, making their way to the next doss house in Canterbury. Occasionally I gave the less unnerving specimens a lift as far as the A2 at Barham. They were usually unwashed, unshorn and unshaved, besides bringing a powerful aroma into the van. I recall one tramp in particular because not only did he not possess a roof to his mouth but he also appeared to be carrying a hot potato of maximum size in it. He talked non-stop for the next twenty minutes. He was, as I imperfectly understood him, telling me about the time he had thrown his wife out of bed five times in a night and broken her leg – or was it the other way round? Or maybe he was chatting about his dear old Auntie in Tipperary.

Another remote churchyard high up on the North Downs had some old farm huts beyond the east end of the churchyard where a red haired girl bred bloodhounds. These creatures set up an unnerving baying every time I was mowing nearby. It took nothing at all to set them off; Conan Doyle's Hound of the Baskervilles could have taken their correspondence course in sinister howling. One of the dogs escaped and came into the churchyard, snuffling round and running in three directions at once, hot on my scent. I gave my imitation of an old grey moss-covered headstone and completely deceived the animal which, baffled, disappeared back through the gate.

I am asked what I mean by churchyard levelling. The idea is simply to make it possible (and easier) to mow a churchyard with machinery. The 'untamed' churchyards could be cut after a fashion by bumping over mounds and curbstones with the Allen Scythe and make some sort of a job but when I began rotary mowing in 1958 it was impossible to use such a machine unless the turf was flat and unencumbered by curbstones or low footstones which could smash up the rapidly revolving knife blade in an instant. Usually there were mounds of varying height which tended to sink down as the earth consolidated – modern mounds can sink as much as two feet below the turf level due partly to insufficient firming as the grave was filled in or the modern use of chipboard coffins which soon disintegrate. Relations might build up the mound again and maybe erect a simple wooden cross or headboard but in old days when few people could read, there was little point in epitaphs. So old graves ended up as long low unidentified hummocks lined up east and west, the wooden inscriptions having long ago rotted away. Then stone headstones started coming into fashion, crosses mounted on plinths, also curbs to mark the grave boundary. The Victorians seem to have been great epitaph raisers. They also went in for 'body stones' long round tapered stones laid between head and footstones which vaguely resembled a trussed up mummy.

Anyone wishing to see a Victorian cemetery at its best (or worst?) has only to visit Highgate cemetery, especially the old side which has, as I recall, 60,000 graves crammed into 35 acres.

It was closed to the public some years ago but I gained access the day before it closed officially by writing to the owners, asking if I might walk round it, being myself the greatest living expert on churchyards in the United Kingdom. A claim they evidently accepted since I was able to spend a whole morning exploring it. This was the time when a gentleman was lurking in the cemetery at night, perfectly convinced that Dracula lived there and he ended up in a police court. There is a creepy area of mausoleums known as the Columbarium and nothing would induce me to spend a night there!

The taller headstones sticking up above the grassy jungles could be seen and avoided but low footstones, 'stone bibles' and curbs lurking in the undergrowth caused much damage even to my tough Allen motor scythe with its reciprocating blades. Ferocious mounds needed cutting by hand and an area of modern mounds and curbs could take a morning to trim by hand and only quarter of an hour by machines.

Verbum sapiendum! From the start of my churchyarding career I was preaching the benefits of levelling churchyards and with the change over to rotary machines in 1958 it became a necessity, although I carried on with the Allen Scythe for many years, dealing with the rougher areas and occasional overgrown lawns for private customers. This work occupied me for most of my winters, the last churchyard to be levelled was Canterbury St Dunstans over 1976 and 1977.

Basically I went round a churchyard with a note book and counted up all the obstacles as under: mounds, footstones, plain curbs, inscribed curbs, stone books and body stones, costing each kind. Headstones were left alone except noting leaning ones to set them upright again. Dealing with these I soon learnt to push the headstones upright rather than pull them towards me. Many were surprisingly fragile where they met the turf and could snap in half.

My tools were very simple. Wheelbarrow, spade, shovel, fourteen pound sledge hammer and a special curved crowbar eight feet long which my blacksmith in Appledore made for me. Originally straight, it went into an S shape at the end working on the very first footstone I jerked out with it. It retained its shape unaltered for the next twenty-four years I used it in churchyards. It still comes in useful to heave out small trees, shrubs and the like which otherwise would entail much digging around the roots.

I dealt with the mounds by slitting the turf down the middle and around the perimeter, then rolling back the turf like a stair carpet. I shovelled away the surplus earth and relaid the strips. The surplus earth was used to level up depressions between mounds, fill in footstone holes and depressions left by the removal of curbstones.

The curbstones received two taps from my sledge hammer to split them into three lengths; these were jerked out with the crowbar and carried away to the boundary wall. Plain curbs usually had a headstone or cross with the epitaphs; the inscribed curbs were taken up and relaid level with the turf.

Body stones were certainly the hardest work and most expensive item since their sheer bulk was such that even my fourteen pound sledge hammer bounced off them but they always caved in eventually. At Ospringe Nicholas and Nigel smashed up forty body stones in a day, knowing that the estimate for that part of the job was eighty pounds and they were congratulating themselves when I pointed out we also had to cart the pieces to the boundary wall (where a farmer's JCB came along with a truck and carted them away).

Sometimes people turned up who had not realised that levelling was in progress, in spite of the advertising on the church door and local papers to obtain the faculty. They agreed with the work when it had been explained to them. Mostly they thought it a good idea to remove the obstacles – provided their own were left! One old man missed his father's footstone (it was behind the headstone) and demanded to know what his father was going to do without it after forty years.

My psychic sense developed specially in the early years since I am sure many of the inhabitants resented having their graves removed or, indeed, having machinery operating instead of a gentle scything. There was sometimes a feeling of active resentment – like that in Appledore church – and sometimes I was made extremely uncomfortable.

I spent three days thirty miles from home levelling a cemetery, staying in the Vicar's caravan for two nights. After the first day I became acutely conscious of one levelled mound which I felt perhaps I should have left. A week after my visit I received a letter from the secretary of the Burial Board, asking me to replace a specific mound and he quoted the grave number, the row and the section of the cemetery. On my next visit I had to work out the reference system (having not bothered about it before) and located the mound – it was the one about which I had felt unhappy. It belonged to an old lady of 104 who had been most insistent on a mound over her grave.

I was working in one small and creepy churchyard, surrounded by thick woods on two sides and open fields on the other – a deserted village site. My mower disturbed a vaulted grave close to the ditch surrounding the church. The following year I was hand-hooking the grass down in this ditch and I became aware of being stared at very intently by some disembodied person standing above me. A feeling of oppression became heavier and heavier to bear until I was on the point of abandoning the work and going home. Then I turned the corner of the church along the east end – and the nightmare vanished as if a switch had been turned off.

There is a difference, I am sure, between the creepy events that occasionally happened to me in churchyards and the majority of hauntings, which I feel are a kind of psychometry. These 'visitations' seemed to be the direct link between my churchyard work and former inhabitants and their spirits came back to bother me – whether they had become aware of my activities in some way or had been 'tipped the wink' by a living person unconsciously sending them a signal, I really have no idea. This feeling of being observed by invisible eyes happened too often for it to be a coincidence.

The other sort of haunting is bound up with the energies concerned with dowsing and they are a form of electrical energy concerned with memory. I mean that some traumatic event in the past causes a rise in the brain voltage and the excess leaks into the surrounding area. Then later, someone comes along, completely relaxed, brain voltage is low and the stored memory is leaked back into the field of the person in it; it might produce a complete re-enactment of the original scene, or just an auditory signal, perhaps even just a scent.

I am sure this is what happened to me three years ago in the little churchyard of St Theresa's chapel outside Northiam, founded by Sheila Kaye-Smith the authoress. I was raking up some grass at the east end of the churchyard and glancing across the field I saw a lady wearing a blue anorak walking with her dog and coming towards me. Maybe she was a hundred yards away and the gate through which she had come was an equal distance behind her.

On my right ran the roadside hedge, there was no way through it. I turned round, raked up some grass for a few seconds, looked back to see where they had reached – and there was no sign of them at all! I had heard of the phrase 'rubbing one's eyes' but never imagined I would do just that. She could not possibly have walked out of sight anywhere.

Much later I was telling the flower lady in the chapel about my experience and only then remembered that years before I used to see a lady coming through the field, walking by the churchyard and leaving the field to enter the lane; I had not seen her for some time. You could say that it was her spirit (and a doggy spirit) – which I had fleetingly observed but in my opinion it was a thought form similar to other hauntings of that nature. The lady did not have to be dead. She might have moved away and her memories of the happy walks she had taken across that field were so intense that they conjured up the thought form. She might then have died but the thought energy carried on. Eventually if no one happened to see her, it would gradually fade away but each sighting puts fresh energy back into the force field, enabling it to continue.

Another residual memory I encountered was outside the tower in Goodnestone churchyard near Canterbury. I was mowing up and down past the tower and had a sudden 'flash' as I passed the doorway. As I carried on behind the machine, a picture built up in my mind of three men standing outside the tower door wearing 18th century costume – silk coats and waistcoats, knee breeches . . . It was like the shutter of a camera clicking and the impression was as brief. It was almost as if the shock of the unexpected vision caused its disappearance.

An odd and creepy experience happened to me one afternoon in early December in Crundale church, remote and high on the North Downs. I had finished my work for the year and as was my custom, on this last visit I went into the church to say a prayer and a farewell until the next season. It was four o'clock and growing dark. I entered the porch and foolishly said aloud: "I wish I could see a ghost!" I could hardly see anything in the church and as I stood in the nave I heard a book drop to the floor. I stood not upon the order of my leaving and was outside in half a dozen huge strides, moving practically at the speed of light! Later I kicked myself for being so timorous but it really was very creepy.

On the subject of ghostly events I can hardly leave out Pluckley village, supposed to be the most haunted area in Kent. I was visiting the village over a number of years on a weekly basis since my 'Victorian eccentric', Miss E.L. Hunter lived there – I wrote about her twelve years ago. I knew the Rector, Revd. Gerald Luckett and he asked me to cut the churchyard. The Dering family vault was under the south chapel, the entrance down steps in the south aisle covered by planking which was very frail and the Rector reckoned it would collapse sooner or later. It did not, but gave way during his successor's incumbency and he pitched down the steps, sustaining injuries; he was never the same man again.

However, an old man used to walk through the churchyard while I was mowing and I asked if he had ever seen a ghost. He told me he had walked through the churchyard for sixty years and 'never seed no ghost'. The churchwarden's sister kept a small shop where I bought my lunches and she told me she had never seen anything, nor did she know of anyone who had seen a ghost. On the other hand, I was mowing Biddenden churchyard one day and a lady stopped to tell me how she and her husband had been driving through the main street at Pluckley past the church and they both stared with astonishment at a figure walking along the pavement. "Did you see what I saw?", one said to the other. And the reply: "Yes, a knight in armour!". Fancy dress or a ghost?

L-R: Admiral Sir Reginald Parry, K.C.B., R.N.(ret), Valentine, Monk, Michael's constant companions in the van travelling to and from churchyards. They do not usually rest on this fine plush curtain, which is just a background for the picture, but they say they would fancy having it permanently as it improves their image.

Goudhurst cemetery, for a long time Michael's responsibility with its beautiful Yew trees, a splendid example of topiary.

Audrey in charge of the two rotary mowers at Westwell cemetery.

Above: *Churchyard consultant "on the job" in Bridge churchyard (1966).*

Right: *Nicholas, Nigel and Beetle Dog working at Stelling churchyard (1964).*

Barham churchyard May 1968: Michael cutting the cow parsley with the Allen scythe, practically hidden.

The Vicar of Sellindge (near Ashford, Kent) looking at a heap of demolished gravestones from his cemetery, which is in process of being levelled. There will be at least twenty tons of broken curbs and concrete slabs to be carted away.

Michael Jack, 33 Albert Road, Hythe, Kent

CHAPTER TWELVE

Dowsing

This leads me into another topic briefly touched on in my last book. Readers may remember a photograph of me, swinging my pendulum over a map looking for tunnels.

A good illustration is a visit I paid to a vicarage garden thirty miles or more away. A local archaeologist friend had asked if I could locate wells in the Vicarage garden and he sent me a sketch map. I drew a half-inch grid on the paper and duly found possible well sites. As an afterthought I asked if there was any silver buried in the garden. To my surprise I located a site on the lawn. Reporting this to my friend, he wrote back and said the church silver had disappeared at the Reformation – the Vicar was most interested! So I visited the Vicarage, duly found the place on the lawn and after removing the turf and digging down twelve inches, swung my pendulum over the hole, there was no reaction, this now happened over the spoil heap. Sifting through this I found the cause of the reaction – it was a hand made copper roofing nail! Searching mentally for silver I evidently picked up copper instead. I was using Lethbridge's long pendulum of 22" for silver. A further effort would doubtless have separated them, carrying a 'witness' of silver – a small piece of silver held with the pendulum – a teaspoon, perhaps. Even so, the fact remains that by swinging my pendulum over a hand drawn map over thirty miles from the site enabled me to pinpoint a small copper nail buried in the soil. I might point out that no one knew about the nail and therefore telepathy was not involved.

In similar vein it is possible to stand over a well and ask the pendulum to gyrate once for every foot of depth. I first tried this over the well in the grounds of Saltwood Castle. There were village rumours of tunnels down the well; one of them went to Westenhanger Castle not far away and was used by Henry II to visit his lady love Rosamund Clifford. I arranged with the owners of the castle, Alan and Jane Clark, to organise a team from my Kent Underground Group to descend the well on an electron ladder and ascertain the truth of the matter.

In fact there were two tunnels forty feet down the well, each about twenty-two feet long and five to six feet high, built of relatively modern bricks. It was reckoned their purpose was to extend the capacity of the well.

It was a good opportunity to test the dowsing and gain the actual depth of the well afterwards. My pendulum said it would be sixty-three feet and it was actually sixty-four. Another well in Smallhythe, outside Tenterden gave a reaction of thirty-four feet and was proved to be thirty-nine. Emboldened by my success I tested the well in Charmian's garden, high above Sandgate Esplanade between Hythe and Folkestone. I said it would be thirty-six feet and dropping down a line showed it to be only twelve!

So why did my dowsing fail? In this sort of work you have to keep the mind completely relaxed, quite indifferent to the result. This can be difficult to achieve; if one has a preconceived idea of the answer then that is what you will find. In the case of Charmian's well I certainly felt that it would be a deep one, being situated so high about the sea level and therefore my preconceived notion overrode the dowsing effect. I have no doubt that a stream of water ran down the hillside twelve feet down

It can be easier to dowse for other people than for oneself, there is not the same mental involvement. I lost my van keys once and was very annoyed because I could not go out. I swung my pendulum over a series of questions – are the keys in the house? In the garage? and so on. The answer given was that the keys were under my courgettes. A search revealed nothing. I tried again – yes, keys are under courgettes. Audrey came home soon afterwards and said she was sorry, had put my van keys in the hall table drawer. Obviously my state of mind precluded any dowsing success.

On the other hand twice I lost my secateurs in the garden and found them both times. Having several professional pairs I was not particularly cross. I took my dowsing rods (made from a metal coat hanger) and walked from the back door up the garden path. The rods pointed straight ahead through the gate at the top, then the right rod turned towards the van. A search under the driving seat revealed the missing secateurs – I had missed them on an earlier search. The second time I used the rods they led me again by the van; one rod pointed towards it, the other pointed to the bonfire. I knew there were secateurs already in the van so I looked into the bonfire heap and soon found the missing secateurs. I was carrying a spare pair to act as a 'witness' of what I was searching for. They have no effect in themselves but kept my mind well concentrated on the object being searched for.

Besides the rods and various pendulums I also use a four foot long piece of metal waterpipe – this is solely for seeking cavities such as tunnels. By approaching the line of tunnel from both sides the width is easily obtained and the tunnels down the well in Saltwood castle were easily dowsed. On reaching the edge of the cavity the pipe will drop down in front of me. The rods cut from a metal coat hanger have the handle piece cut off and the remainder cut in half, which gives two straightened sections about twenty – one inches long. I bent a handle about five inches long, leaving sixteen inches of rod to point forward, ready for reactions. Some people slip the handles into old ball pen cases to enable an easier swivelling action but in any sort of a wind the rods can go haywire, I just adjust my grip round the handles according to conditions.

Usually the rods will cross over on meeting with the object of the search but this by no means always the case. Both rods may move left or right if a 'track' is being followed or if something enters in from left or right then that rod alone will react – as with my secateurs. On coming up to church altars, standing stones and stone circles the rods swing outwards, presumably showing a spiral or circular force passing round in front of me. So approaching another person's body there will be a crossing over reaction as you enter that person's electrical force field which could be from two to six inches wide.

I was asked to find a possible water source in a field; was given a sketch map of the area with any features marked on it – there were none in this case. I put on my usual grid and failed to find any water streams. I did obtain a solid block of reactions which I could not understand at all and a later visit to the site proved the reactions were caused by a small vineyard!

There is a photograph of me in the first book being 'pushed' off a stone in the Castlerigg stone circle near Keswick. I was watched by a holidaymaker with great interest; he wanted to try it himself and positioned his girlfriend to take his picture as he fell off. I regret to say that nothing happened! Probably he was so tensed up with excitement that the relatively weak power could not operate.

Ever since the Castlerigg circle I have been anxious to test the stones in Cornwall. In spring of 1991 we travelled around the western part of Cornwall, so redolent of Celtic settlers and we found two standing stones and a stone circle quite close to each other on the road from Penzance towards Lands End, just past Trewoofe on the B3315. The stone nearest the road was surely twelve feet high and upright, its fellow nearby leaned over. My first thought was that the second stone had leaned over during the centuries but a glance at Tom Graves' book Needles of Stone told me that they were placed at an angle, pointing to at least two underground water sources whereas the vertical stones are situated directly over them.

Audrey and I put our arms round the vertical stone and were pushed off after a short time; the rods reacted by moving outward. The stone circle gave a similar reaction: as we entered between any two stones the rods reacted outward – just a gentle movement. These stone are very evocative of the remote past. I ask myself why they were built at a cost of so much labour. Often in lonely places, these stone have been standing sentinel over generation after generation of people, back for two, three or more thousand years. Still the stones stand there, seemingly immortal if not disturbed by society – as many indeed have been.

Who raised them and why did they go to such colossal labour? What did they do with the power that had been generated? Graves states that the power comes from underground water springs and sources at the centre of a stone circle . Did they build up the power by dancing round the circles and stones? He also says that some dowsers have actually sustained electric shocks from testing stones or ended up with migraine headaches which took quarter of an hour to disperse. We visited Chrysauster the stone age village up on the hills between Penzance and St Ives and we found some active stones there. At one point Audrey wandered off and I was alone. By myself I was conscious of a distinct feeling of creepiness as though I was not alone in the hutments.

Mediaeval church altars also give this reaction. There seems to be a spiral force round each altar and standing with the hands each side of it will usually mean you are pushed off one way or another and the rods give the outward reaction. I adopt my dowsing stance – a kind of meditation – and await events. After a while I feel a gentle pressure, one hand becomes heavier and the other starts slipping along the altar top. Eventually I have to stand back or I would end up on the floor. It is supposed to be strongest on days before new and full moon so there is some kind of earth current involved although I suspect that centuries of worship concentrated on the sanctuary may have something to add.

Churches are often built over former pagan sites – St Augustine was told to Christianise them so I wonder if the altar was placed where the pagan rites took place. So that was the first objective and the church built round this. I suppose this knowledge was lost eventually, and churches were built where ever seemed convenient without reference to the character of the site. For example, the ruined Coventry cathedral is very much alive but the modern cathedral built at right angles has no 'life' at all. Canterbury cathedral, for example, is an expression not only of the Christian faith but of something far older; I am told there is hardly a true right angle in the building. and I obtain reactions there which are quite inexplicable in normal terms.

Another curious dowsing feature are 'track lines'. These can be dowsed on a map as 'tunnels' but when the depth is sought the tunnels are so shallow – maybe eighteen to twenty-four inches they are obviously not tunnels. It has been found that regular walking from A to B will produce a kind of 'memory' and this gets picked up by the dowser. For example, only five days ago I was asked to investigate

Above: Merry Maidens: Audrey standing in centre over water source. (Cornwall 1991).

Below: Michael testing stone circle with rods (they opened out passing through two stones), (near Matlock 1992).

tunnels under Chilham churchyard running possibly from a splendid old house due south east of the church. This was, very long ago, the parsonage. My map dowsing of the house and garden picked up a line running from the house across the garden and beyond the churchyard wall to the church. Obviously a 'tunnel' was the first thought. But trying for depth proved it to be about twenty inches down, so it was not a tunnel. When Audrey and I went Chilham last Sunday I tested the site; it was obviously where the old parsons had walked from their back door over to the church; I looked for a gate in the wall or a blocked gateway. There was none, therefore the trackway was established before the wall was built. I picked up another line running from the west end of the house and curving round towards the church. We were taken into the cellar – this house must be at least five hundred years old – and where my map dowsing had predicted a possible tunnel, there were all the signs of a blocked tunnel in the same position. My water pipe test suggested there was a cavity behind the end wall of this area. The line could be established in the churchyard and the depth trial suggested thirteen feet below the turf. Quite different depth reaction from the trackline. Furthermore the President of the British Society of Dowsers was with us and he confirmed my findings independently. He said that even regular sheep tracks across fields will show up on a map or on site. And cattle runs also.

A final comment on power lines across the country carrying high voltage current. Recently there have been reports of people living under these lines suffering from a variety of ailments, including migraines. I can well believe this, having walked under power lines holding my rods; they not only cross over sharply but went further and turned backwards.

In my earlier dowsing days I did not realise that a reaction would be obtained from 'track lines' as well as from tunnels. Faversham churchyard was in my care for over quarter of a century. Over the churchyard wall on the north side of the church had been the former abbey, founded by King Stephen, of which not a trace remained. When a new school was built on the site, the foundations came to light and the builders uncovered the old burial ground with skeletons still remaining laid out in rows.

I had heard rumours of a tunnel running under the churchyard between abbey and church and a dowsing back and forth gave me a line of reactions which seemed to confirm the story. Convinced that I had the line of the tunnel, I approached the Vicar and he kindly gave me permission to excavate a trench near the church (away from likely burials) to establish the truth of the rumour. I enlisted the help of my son-in-law Peter Heselden and between us we dug down twelve or fourteen feet through the sandy soil close to the north wall of the chancel – we found absolutely nothing!

Years later I realised that my reactions were caused by a 'track line' created by the monks as for centuries they moved between abbey and church. Had I then known about testing for depth, I am sure it would have been not more than two feet, probably less.

Interestingly, following the uncovering of the monkish graves, a well known local resident was reported as having seen a line of ghostly monks processing across the churchyard about nine o'clock one night. Unfortunately his credibility was destroyed soon afterwards when he was involved in a homosexual scandal and served a prison sentence. After that, nobody believed in his story any more!

The pendulum is a useful tool in my garden work and there is always one in my van – a piece of larva pebble from the slope of the volcano Vesuvius, which we have climbed on two occasions. The purpose of the pendulum is to determine which way to plant anything, whether a cabbage or a flowering shrub.

The logic of the exercise should be obvious. Plants have been growing at home or purchased from a garden centre and ideally they should be planted in the same direction – viz., if the main growth is north and south then they need replanting north and south and not east and west. In the latter case they will need adjust themselves and time is lost.

But how to detect which way to plant them? I hold the shrub or whatever gently in my left hand in the suggested position and swing a short pendulum over it – say about five inches and mentally ask the plant if it will be 'happy' in that position. If the pendulum swings positively (clock-wise for me) planting takes place without delay. Or there may be a negative reaction (anti-clockwise), in which case I twist the plant a quarter turn and ask again . . . and again until the reaction is positive. If you obtain only negative reactions then you know the plant will not flourish there.

Anyone can check for this gift by swinging a pendulum over a house plant, noting the gyration and then turning the pot round at least ninety degrees. The majority of people especially those with 'green fingers' will obtain a different reaction. For boxes of seedlings I swing my pendulum over the box and move it around until the reaction is positive and then take out each little seedling and put it in to face the same way as in the box.

One amusing incident at my expense must be related. I was about to plant out a box of Petunia plantlets in my Hythe High Street beds in front of Portex House, and was swinging my pendulum when two men passing by stopped and asked what I was doing. I explained about the dowsing and without comment they walked on. But after they reached the old post office ten yards away, I heard a voice within my ear, transmitted by my hearing aid. "He is quite mad!!". I glanced up but they had moved on. If they looked back at me I would have stuck up two fingers in a derisory comment.

I expect many readers, reading about my account of sleeping over running water at Enbrook Manor House, Folkestone, dismissed the whole affair as a figment of my imagination. After eighteen months in the house I started sleeping badly, exhaustion at night, continual sweating and nearly collapsing in church one Sunday. I had read somewhere of the perils of 'black streams' and sleeping over water streams and dowsing our bedroom showed a thin stream running underneath our bed. We moved the bed away and I gradually recovered – but to some extent still feel the effects twenty-two years later. I mentioned this to the secretary of the British Society of Dowsers and he confirmed my fears, saying I might eventually had died, had we not moved away from the influence. The sequel came twelve years later. The people who bought our house chose the same position for their bed as we did originally. Later Annagret began sleeping badly, sweating etc. – all the symptoms from which I had suffered. Our former neighbours lent her a copy of my book; she read about the running water business and realised it was happening to her as well. Her husband was only slightly affected – Audrey never was. So they moved the bed away and once again all was well.

I met the new owner not long ago and asked if he had noticed anything upsetting. He had not, but I know he had installed complete central heating and maybe the copper piping has earthed the influence.

I had an interesting encounter with a young Gipsy girl when about to start a grass cutting job. She stopped by my van and asked if I would buy a roll of lace which she had made. The price was five pounds. I told her I had not five pounds in my purse – a long fabric one I used to carry the small change from mowing lawns. I opened the top and showed her the contents – shillings and copper coins. "There is not five pounds' worth of change here" I told her. She looked directly at me and said: " There is a five pound note at the bottom of your purse". This was true so I admitted the fact and handed it over in exchange for the lace. She told me we had been through a difficult time recently – Audrey's mother suffered from Alzheimers Disease and had died. She looked at my van and told me I would me changing it very shortly. I bought another van three weeks later. One hears of gipsy second sight and here was a good example of it.

CHAPTER THIRTEEN

My unusual Victorian Client

The rural dean of a group of parishes high up on the North Downs became a keen protagonist of my churchyarding activities.

He was also Vice-Dean of Canterbury cathedral and his influence gained me many clients in his rural deanery. He lived in Doddington and the first village I came to after turning off the A20 was Wychling. It was hardly even a hamlet, the village having vanished centuries before. The church stood entirely alone across a field, surrounded on two sides by a thick wood and more fields on the north side. In the churchyard was a large vault which contained the remains of the Norton family. The Reverend Norton had been Vicar there in the early part of this century; he, his wife, son and two daughters were all in the vault. The remaining daughter Muriel Norton still lived in the old Vicarage a few yards down the road from the church, and I was soon asked to call on her because she needed help keeping down her garden grass. She had maybe three acres of jungle behind the house and literally no-one able or willing to cut it.

So I called on her to see what she wanted and and I came to know and have a great affection for the old lady. She lived entirely alone in this huge rambling dilapidated old house. There was no mains water, no electricity, no gas and no form of central heating. Behind the house was a fearsome jungle of grass, nettles, thistles, docks and all the weeds occasioned by years of neglect. Bordering the house was a lawn the size of two tennis courts with a gigantic Monkey Puzzle tree in the centre. At one side was a similar sized area formerly tennis courts, bounded on all sides by a huge overgrown yew hedge which must have been ten feet thick and tree height. Behind all this were further areas of desolation which Miss Norton was not bothered about. Indeed, I was thankful not to be encumbered with it; even the Allen Scythe would have found it hard work cutting through growth seven feet high!

The old lady wanted me to call twice a year when I cut Wychling churchyard before or after I had done Doddington and cut the two main 'lawns'; she would clear the hay herself – she must have been seventy then and a small frail old lady! It would be a relatively easy job compared to churchyards, being flat. Even so, my heart sank when I surveyed it and my first impulse was to decline the work, there was more than enough to do already with the growing churchyard connections. However, I decided I had better help her, once the top growth had been cut down it should be just a matter of mowing up and down ; the only obstacles were huge ant heaps into which the Allen Scythe stuck its knife fingers and stalled. The job usually meant between two and three hours of very hard work.

Miss Norton was a very determined old lady and she decided I must have a Good Lunch; my statement that I usually ate a pork pie and potato crisps was greeted with horror! Around one o'clock on the first mowing visit she came out and called me into the house. My lunch was ready and she had heated up a jug of hot water for a wash. So I entered through the conservatory into the house and it was like entering a time warp, stepping back fifty years. A big hall, hung with large oil paintings barely visible in the dim light – most of the shutters were closed. A kitchen with stone-flagged floor; a tin basin with a hot water jug besides it awaited me. The water came from the roof, collected into large tanks somewhere on the premises. She cooked on oil stoves and the illumination was by candles and paraffin lamps. She wanted no help in the house and saw to everything herself, including cooking my hot lunch.

She conducted me into the dining room, where she had laid a place for me and then she went out and returned with a plate of soup, followed by hot sausages with baked beans – and stone-cold mashed potatoes. Already on the table was a dish of tinned peaches and cream with orangeade to drink and a pot of tea afterwards.

It was all very strange; my deafness made it a fairly silent world (I had no hearing aid at that time and could just about manage without one, in normal conversations), but this silence was quite oppressive. Miss Norton had disappeared but she popped in occasionally to make sure I was happy and had enough to eat.

I glanced round the dining room as I ate and it dawned slowly on me that everything in the room was covered in a layer of dust – not the usual sort of dust of a week or two but of layer upon layer of a thick dust gathered over very many years. I looked more carefully at my plate and saw that it was covered with as thick a layer of dust as everything else in the room – wiping my finger round the edge left the white mark of the plate beneath. Oddly, it did not trouble me in the least. There was a dim light in the dining room; Miss Norton had opened only one set of shutters, but I could see two grandfather clocks, a Broadwood grand piano, an Indian fan as used by a 'punkah wallah'. On the mantlepiece was a silver mounted horse's hoof inscribed with the owner's name and 'Grand National 1902'.

After Miss Norton came in again I told her that someone had come to the door, looked in and gone away again. I thought we were alone in the house. "Oh yes we are," she said brightly. "That would have been my last sister – she died eighteen months ago". She explained that all the members of her family had returned after their funerals to reassure her that life went on elsewhere . . .

After lunch I tried the Broadwood but it was terribly out of tune. She took me upstairs to another Broadwood grand but that was even more horribly out of tune than the downstair one! Striking say, middle C resulted in a jangle of sound as all three strings were out of tune with each other.

I called on Miss Norton and cut the grass for many years and enjoyed my chats with her, always being given a good lunch. Occasionally I varied my round and cut Doddington first and then I was given tea in the sitting room – buttered scones or crumpets and two hard boiled eggs. The egg cups, bless her, were encrusted with years of ancient egg yolks, layer upon layer and this was a trifle off-putting. I reasoned that the eggs were fresh so the appearance of the eggs cups did not matter. Anyway, as I said, I had an affection for the old lady. Being somewhat of an eccentric myself I enjoyed chatting to another one. She appeared to look forward to my visits and the last thing I would have done would be to cause her any embarrassment.

Towards the end of her life I called and found her looking very thin – almost wasted away – she was a small and thin old lady in any case – and I was shocked at her appearance. She said she had had a fall but refused to call her doctor or any friends since she had heard the hamlet had been hit by virulent influenza. She decided to cut herself off from the outside world from possible infection and for two or three weeks she had subsisted, as I understood her, mostly on cake. Like my other eccentric customer, old Miss Hunter and as fiercely independent, she wanted no 'outside interference' in her affairs and would certainly have made short shrift of any social worker foolish enough to call.

Eventually she had to move into a small private Home in Faversham, where I visited her shortly before her death, on one my visits to Faversham churchyard. I was deeply shocked to see how she had deteriorated; the Muriel Norton I had known for so many years had gone and only this thin shadow remained, barely able to recognise me but still pleased with my visit.

She used to have a dog named Harry, who spent much of his time chained up outside the conservatory door and I always heard him barking furiously as I brought the mower down the drive. Eventually Harry died and it was in keeping with Miss Norton and the rest of her family that he returned after he had been buried in the garden. She complained bitterly that he had taken to sleeping on the sofa in the sittingroom, thereby preventing her from using it. However, by my next visit she had solved Harry's haunting proclivities by the simple expedient of laying a heavy concrete slab on top of his grave. That, she told me with satisfaction, kept Harry down below!

Miss Muriel Norton, a Victorian Eccentric.

CHAPTER FOURTEEN

Underground

Anyone who knows me and something of my interests will be expecting to read a little about our trips into caves, tunnels, drains, wartime bunker headquarters.

I must admit I came to this hobby quite late in life, in my fifties when I saw a meeting of the William Pengelly Caving Trust advertised to be held in London in the early nineteen seventies. My banker churchyarding friend John expressed an interest and we were enthralled by the speakers and the slides they showed of their explorations, especially those in the south-eastern parts of the country. I joined the society and my first trip with them was down a dene hole at Grays, Essex. It entailed climbing down an electron ladder into a seventy feet deep vertical hole. (The electron ladder is the modern equivalent of the old rope ladder, being made of thin steel wire with six inch wide treads of aluminium and sections can be bolted together, giving any length of ladder).

Dene holes were an entirely new concept to me. Basically it is a vertically excavated circular pit, anything from twenty to seventy feet deep, from four to six feet diameter and it was dug in order to get at the underlying chalk which was an important part of farming many centuries ago. It was brought to the surface in baskets and spread on the land – especially clay land to sweeten it. Since transport was impossibly difficult in the old days, farmers tended to sink their shafts near the fields which were to have the chalk applied and so these pits appear in large numbers in parts of the country where there is underlying chalk – as in many parts of Kent and near London in Bexley, for example. The usual plan was for the vertical shaft to be extended in a clover leaf design once the chalk had been reached. The caverns did not extend far, being governed by the requirements of the workers mining the chalk. They shovelled the chalk into baskets which were drawn along and up the shaft by ropes operated from above. This is explaining dene holes in the simplest fashion to show what sort of adventures I was launching into.

I asked a local friend to come with me – Roger Blackman, then maintenance engineer at the Hythe Portex factory. I had started the garden and grass cutting contact at Portex before Roger appeared. Soon after his arrival he decided that I ought to be organised into the factory system. He complained to his secretary Ann Douglas that "We have this gardener coming and going, we don't know his movements; we don't know what he is going to do nor what it will cost. We must plan a routine for his activities". Ann had been dealing with me for some time and she explained to Roger what I was like and how I worked. Roger told me – much later – that he gave up the whole idea instantly!

On our arrival at the Dene hole site we found ourselves faced with two dene holes. Originally the entire area had been excavated but all the other shafts had been filled in, leaving these two and down at the bottom there was an absolute labyrinth of tunnels as all the old workings had been joined up by tunnelling between the cloverleaf excavations.

Roger and I regarded the first hole with absolute horror and moved on quickly to the other entry which looked less intimidating – even if only marginally so. The first shaft involved negotiating a tree trunk sticking out ten feet from the surface and we were cheerfully told of one lady who went down and got in such a panic that she was unable to climb out again and had to be hauled out 'like a sack of potatoes' as one experienced member put it! This did nothing at all for our confidence, by then pretty well at rock bottom, hence moving to the other shaft.

By the time our turn had come to make the descent we were both regretting ever having come to Grays at all but having announced our intention of going down – in low hoarse voices, we did not wish to lose face by backing out.

My turn came . . . I was told that after putting my toes into the electron ladder rung, I must bend back my knee, thereby bringing the ladder away from the side of the shaft, enabling the other foot to slide into the rung below. Also to hold the ladder from behind with the palms of my hands facing towards me; this gave a better and less tiring grip. I had a life-line tied round my middle which was belayed back to an experienced caver who in turn was roped to a tree trunk behind him. The rope passed round his back, across to his chest and in the event of my falling off the ladder he would bring his arm smartly up to his chest and arrest my descent. Perhaps the rope was passed behind the tree before it was taken. If no tree is available then heavy crowbars were driven and used as anchor points.

Anyway, off I set and immediately forgot all the good advice. I took one foot from the rung and couldn't get it into the next position, then I lost the other footing and found myself hanging by my hands alone with a seventy foot vertical drop below me! I was in a state of absolute mortal terror – never so frightened in my life. All right to know that someone had hold of the line supporting me – but supposing he sneezed at the precise moment I urgently required his services? Then the counsel about bending back the knee came back to mind, I managed to wriggle one toe into the rung, the foot followed; I bent back my knee and immediately gained the routine. Down I went, with the steady pull of the lifeline going down with me.

Once down below, Roger and I had a splendid time crawling through a maze of tunnels, some of them a flat-out crawl through an eighteen inch high passage. There must have been about twenty of us down there and camera flash guns firing non-stop.

The time came to climb out again. The life-line was lowered and tied round my waist, I caught hold of the ladder, placed one foot in the bottom rung and heaved upwards. The end of the ladder shot away from me until I was almost horizontal and the ladder began revolving slowly round and round. Another panic started setting in – it looked as if I would never get out alive . . . The sky looked to be the size of an old fashioned threepenny piece infinitely far above my head.

However, the knee-bending trick worked again, brought the ladder almost vertical and slowly I started climbing up.

After I had climbed up fifty feet or so, looked up and realised I had another twenty feet to climb, panting at the rate of fifty to the minute, an arrival at the top seemed highly improbable. But the life-line was pulling gently upwards waiting for me to resume my ascent until I was finally lying down on the grass, watching Roger coming up. He shared the same feelings of terror and conviction that he would never make it either. But sitting side by side, having a much needed thermos of coffee and some sandwiches, we realised that although we had indeed been in states of terror yet, looking back on it we actually enjoyed the experience!

From my contacts with the William Pengelly cavers I met members of Subterranea Britannica with contacts all over the country and extending into Europe. Later our friend Rod le Gear started the Kent Underground research Group, a much more local organisation but some of the members have a country-wide reputation for experience and know-how. They are always being called in when ever a new hole appears somewhere – sometimes a dene hole, sometimes a housing estate has been built over a long-forgotten mine – chalk or ragstone usually and the ground subsides into an old tunnel or shaft. Dene holes were often backfilled when no longer used by throwing down an old tree trunk, some brush wood and levelled off with earth. Years later the wood has rotted and falls to the bottom, taking the back-filled soil with it. So another pit appears in somebody's back garden! Often there are no records of these old mines or pits.

With Subterranea Britannica we have a summer weekend all over the country exploring old slate and copper mines in Wales, ragstone mines, derelict mines under Box Hill near Bath – where a distant rumble means a bit more roof has fallen in and we hoped we'd still get out! Lead mines in the Yorkshire Dales, diving underneath shops in Nottingham to discover cavernous cellars cut out of the sandstone.

"Why on earth do you and Audrey want to go down those nasty dirty and dangerous holes?" is a common query. Like mountains, the answer is the same: "Because they are there".

Our underground groups travelling around the country in cars or mini-buses differ from ordinary motorists. At the slightest sign of a tunnel, culvert or interesting hole in the ground, our convoy comes to a halt and we all pile out, donning hard hats, collecting torches, cameras, flash guns and pursue the structure with enthusiasm.

Audrey's first introduction underground took place early in my acquaintance with Subterranea Britannica. An expedition was advertised in a news letter giving details of a meeting on the A22 outside Godstone, just north of the M25 interchange. Under the A22 dual carriageway lies an abandoned ragstone mine with miles of tunnels extending in a wide area. There is an entrance under a manhole cover (normally locked), which gave access to a forty foot shaft with climbing irons inserted in the side of the concrete down pipe. On this occasion something was jammed and we had to go in by what looked like a rabbit hole.

To enter the mine we had to dive down this hole head-first, it required a flat-out crawl first down, then up and then down again, a sort of U-bend, finally sliding down a slope into the mine proper. Not the sort of venture anyone with claustrophobia would contemplate. Of course, once down in the mine with thirty other people, all with torches, helmet lamps or flood lights there was plenty of light and a good feeling of common interest and fellowship among our members.

Audrey was the last person to go down and she regarded this 'nasty little hole' with absolute horror; there was no way she could face it and said as much to the elderly gentleman in overalls standing behind her. He was Mr. Gardiner and in fact he was the mine owner. He said he had not intended going down on this trip but he would go first and lead her down the 'rabbit hole'; once past the U-bend she would find it perfectly easy and she would find it well worth while. Which she did and since then has had no qualms about wriggling through some very unpleasant little holes. I was grateful to Mr Gardiner – he taught me the use of a metre of water pipe as a dowsing tool.

We have enjoyed two holidays in Sorrento, Italy and on the second visit we were able to establish contact with an Italian professor in Naples through the good offices of Sylvia Beamon, the chairman of Subterranea Britannica; she had suggested he might be able to take us underground somewhere in the area. So by arrangement we met him, his secretary and her cousin – Michela and Claudia – and a few others. We motored up the slopes on which Naples is built and went through a heavy iron doorway into a perfectly fantastic underground world of enormous caves underneath the city. You could certainly put a church inside some of the caverns, maybe even a small cathedral. The rock is called Tufta and is a volcanic product which the Italians found was excellent for building centuries ago, so much of Naples is built of this stone. These caverns are not open to the public; they told us another series of quarried caverns further up the slope.

When we came out of the caverns, Michela and Claudia offered us a drive around the city, in a friend's car. It was the most terrifying ride we have ever enjoyed! The Italians are mad drivers anyway, swooping out of side roads without signalling or waiting. We noticed in Sorrento there seemed more cars with collision damage than there were without impacts. The girls said that if you could drive in Naples you can drive anywhere in the world. We were inclined to agree – until we spent a week in Rome the following week!

We found ourselves driving along a narrow street just about wide enough for three cars to pass carefully. In this street there were market stalls set up on both sides of the road, cars and vans parked by the stalls and it was a continual battle of wills between opposing drivers about who gave way first. Hooting went on non-stop, of course – after all, the French and Italians hoot at red traffic lights to make them turn green. And apart from the opposing traffic, practically at a standstill most of the time, we had the ubiquitous scooter dodging in and out with careless regard for the paintwork. In fact our driver friend said he would never try it again!

There is a tussle within my mind between enthusiasm for diving underground and my imagination – which is vivid and tends to run amok. Some of our members have crawled into caves and tunnels undisturbed since they were formed centuries or thousand of years ago. I have asked them if they did not fear the possibility of getting trapped down below. They said they never thought about it why should things change just because they were down there? I wondered whether maybe their movements, a cough or sneeze might disturb a delicately balanced rock, to fall and block off their escape. They never seemed to imagine such a possibility. I recall Shakespeare when he wrote: "And as imagination bodies forth the form of things unknown . . ." Potholing is not for me!

I read of one explorer down a pothole who began to lower himself into a cleft in the rock and in so doing dislodged a pebble which rolled down vertically and jammed his ankle against the rock. It proved impossible to extricate him. It was impossible to amputate his leg which was entirely down the rift and after some days he died.

We visited slate mines in Wales, again like Naples with vast church-like caverns and it was staggering to realise it had all been cut away by hand and not only that but with only the dimmest of lights – candles stuck on the miners' cloth caps with clay and maybe working up swaying ladders thirty feet in the darkness. As indeed were the Naples caverns excavated.

Michael in a tight fix, looking unhappy but enjoying every second – even the terrifying descent (but that was after it was all over!!)

(Dene Holes, Grays, Essex)

...tting the wire ladder together.   (Dene Holes)

Game old birds, Clearwell, Iron Ore Mine, Forest of Dean. (June 1993).

CHAPTER FIFTEEN

The Cathedral Drain

A really splendid underground adventure concerned Canterbury cathedral. In 1978 the Marlowe car park was excavated to reveal parts of the Roman city and a notice on the site mentioned The Great Drain running round the cathedral. This sounded like my cup of tea and I wrote to the Dean and Chapter asking if I might be allowed to investigate it. To show my complete respectability I quoted friendship with Archbishop Donald Coggan and Archdeacon Neil Nye, both of whom had also been at Merchant Taylors. Evidently convinced of my trustworthiness I was told to meet the Clerk of the Works, Brian le Mar, in his office and his foreman Mr. Sims would conduct me to the Drain. I had only to sign a paper accepting responsibility for anything that happened to me on my visit.

Mr. Sims had little knowledge of the Great Drain and no one seemed to have explored it recently. In the Dark Entry on the north side of the cathedral there is a large detailed map of the cathedral and the former monastic sites round it and the Drain is clearly marked. It started about south-west of the entrance into the cathedral where most tourists go, passed to the right of this SW porch, went all along the south side under the grass, round the east end of the cathedral, along under the Deanery garden. It went due west under the south side of Green Court, in the centre of Kings School, to turn north at the far west side to go along under the paving stones, past the Kings School library and its Roman staircase to end up hard by the north wall. Originally it must have discharged into the city moat but now presumably into the city sewer system.

But all this I only learnt much later. Mr. Sims took me to the final manhole by the north wall, pulled up the cover and I looked down with ravenous interest at a ten foot shaft with a a round drainage hole at the bottom. The shaft had climbing staples let into the brickwork and it was easy to descend and find myself within the brick-lined tunnel, just high enough to allow me to crouch almost on hands and knees. It was wondrously muddy silt and water down there, my feet sank several inches into the sludge. I had with me my fluorescent caving lamp, camera and flash gun and I crawled up a few yards and took some photographs but mindful of Mr. Sims waiting patiently above me – he did not display any interest in joining me in my muddy environment! I did not delay too long.

Six months later, having studied the Dark Entry map by photographing it and having enlargements made from my negative, I organised a proper expedition to see how far we could crawl up and down the Drain. Nicholas came with me, also Roger. This time we opened a manhole halfway along the west side pavement and shinned down a drop of eight feet into muddy water and silt. First we crawled south towards the cathedral – it was atrociously dirty and headroom was so restricted that parts became a hands and knees crawl. While my first inspection had proved the tunnel to be brickwork, this section was really old and a close examination showed it must be the original Norman construction; the building blocks proved to be – not stone – but chalk. Jet black after centuries of use, yet a scratch with a knife blade proved the gleaming whiteness of the chalk – fantastic! Amazing to realise it had been built around nine hundred years earlier. This chalk did not extend very far towards the north end; extensive repairs had obviously been carried out in Tudor times – my first descent showed it was five hundred years old brickwork .

Before we started crawling up the Drain, I tied the end of a ball of string to the manhole and let it out as we moved up the tunnel. At the far end we were very disappointed to end up within another manhole; the Drain entered it from the east as a round pipe a foot diameter; the cover over our heads was immoveable. Laying the string out on the pavement above showed that the manhole was overlaid by tarred macadam pathway. The Drain was full of tree roots hanging down from the roof, growing through the brickwork in search of the water.

We climbed down the manhole again to see how far we could crawl along the final stretch past the Kings School library. The level of the silt began to rise until it almost reached the roof and the hands and knees crawl became a flat-out wriggle. As we knew where we were going to end up there seemed little point in carrying on so we wriggled out in reverse – a totally exhausting business, especially when encumbered with a lantern and a camera with flash gun attachment.

That concluded the first part of my explorations and I had no plans to go down again. But not long afterwards I received a message from the Dean's wife, Dr. Esther de Waal, a noted historian and writer in her own right. She had heard about my activities and asked me to call and inspect a tunnel in the Deanery garden. From my study of the map of the Drain I felt this was probably a part of it; on the other hand it might be something quite different and no one could say where we might end up! I met Esther in her Deanery and we laid a plan to explore her tunnel the following week.

So Audrey and I went to the Deanery and Esther took us to a rose bed in the garden, I pulled up the manhole cover and there was another utterly fascinating brick tunnel eight feet below us. The three of us went down a borrowed ladder, her son John also came along and first we crawled westwards underneath the Dark Entry passage between Kings School Green Court and the cathedral. Here the Drain was almost twice the width of my earlier tunnels and built of Tudor brick. But soon we came to a brick wall with a one foot diameter drainpipe set in it – obviously the end of that pipe I had found earlier in the western section of the Drain. It seems that this area suffered in the raids on the city in 1942. This section took in the monks' 'Necessarium' and carried away the results of their ablutions so it must have been damaged; in any case the heating system for the cathedral and all The Precinct properties was built in this area – some is actually under the lawn and it was paid for by Canadian subscriptions. There is no trace of the Necessarium now.

We retraced our footsteps to the man-hole (literally, we sank several inches into the silt at each step) and headed east to see where we ended up. This really excited me . . . my imagination pictured us travelling right underneath the city and maybe coming up by the Castle. I led the way with my fluorescent torch, then Esther with a torch followed by Audrey and her son, who also carried a torch. I had tied a string to the manhole as before and just as well I did so. John found himself unable to continue and fled back to the manhole with his torch, leaving Audrey in pitch darkness and she only retraced her path by holding on to my string and groping her way out.

But I knew nothing of this. I pressed on eagerly; the tunnel was about four feet wide, sometimes five feet high, then suddenly descending to three feet – it was fortunate I had my caving helmet on – I had spare ones for the other three. Stumbling through pools of water, inches deep, soft muddy silt; the passage turned and twisted until I had no idea at all in which direction I was heading.

Then the roof came down to thirty inches and it became a hands and knees crawl. Ahead of me I saw a faint gleam of daylight and after some minutes I found some holes in the side of the Drain and peering through, realised at once where I had arrived. Some weeks earlier, on my first visits, I had seen work going on outside the south side of the cathedral by St Anselm's chapel. There had been dampness here, the ground was excavated and a limestone wall was built eventually which acted as a wick, to draw up and evaporate the water. The downpipe from the roof was directed into the Drain. As far as I could tell the water found its own way in naturally, in similar fashion to land drains laid under fields; there are no cemented joints, the water enters through between each pipe. Incidentally this area was formerly the monks' cemetery and their bones stuck out here and there.

I began to wonder where everybody else had got to. Then far away in the distance I saw a faint glimmer of a torch, brave Esther was on her way and soon we were crouched side by side debating our next move. We decided to return by the same route, not then being aware that two man-holes were ahead of where we were kneeling and we could have crawled on another fifty or so yards and pushed up a manhole cover; it would entail a flatout wriggle since the tunnel was less than two feet high. I have a photograph of Esther standing in this man-hole and her knees are still visible above the lawn. The reason why she was so far behind me was due to her losing one of her boots in the wet muddy silt. In spite of the damp conditions down the Drain the air was perfectly fresh and my camera lens never misted up with condensation. (It did on another occasion after some rain, the water was several inches deep under the Deanery garden area. I managed to have two flash guns put out of action as well as the condensation on the lens being too severe to wipe away; in addition I lost two re-chargeable batteries while fiddling with the flash guns trying to persuade them to work. As far as I know the batteries are still down there!).

I paid several later visits down this part of the Drain to add to my photographs; one friend noticed a circular tunnel maybe three feet or less in diameter and crawled off up it while I waited in the main passage. Eventually he returned – crawling backward since he came to a dead end and was unable to turn round. With him he brought a long steel spike and half a coconut shell. My churchyarding friend John came once and we agreed that the flat-out part of the Drain was hardly the place to stage a heart attack! How would the patient be brought out?

The circular culvert mentioned just now must have drained the now-ruined infirmary and chapel immediately to the north east of the cathedral. Around the area the Drain was not far below the ground and my friends could hear people conversing above them. There was a terrible temptation to give a bubbling scream and shout NO NO NO!, emitting cackles of manic laughter. It would have required a collaborator above ground to record tourists' reactions on film! As it was, when our parties pushed up the south side man-hole and presented their muddy selves to the tourists it caused the latter some astonishment.

Esther had remarked on the superb quality of the underground Tudor brickwork, so beautifully laid and enduring so well even after five hundred years of service. I looked up my Dart's History of Canterbury Cathedral (1726) – which I bought at an Appledore auction sale for half a crown in 1948. I found an entry under Lives of the Priors, Thomas Goldstone II in 1480. "About this time there was a great resort of people to Our Lady's chappell in the crypt but by reason of several springs the water generally flowed in there, so that the Devotees could not without difficulty resort to it. He therefore made a famous Aqueduct or Drain which goes from the church gate, cross the churchyard to the church and under the foundations of it."

In a very dry summer the course of the Drain may be traced running under the turf to the east side of the path leading to the main tourist entrance, the south west porch.

I conducted a party of Subterranea Britannica enthusiasts down the Drain some years ago by arrangement with Esther. She was not able to be present and left it to her husband to do the honours. He obviously thought we were all quite mad, wishing to enter into such a dank, smelly, muddy claustrophobic environment! After we had completed our tour and climbed back on the Deanery lawn we counted heads and found one member was missing. We pulled up the Deanery manhole – no sign of him. We went to the manholes on the south lawn and had them up – no sign of him. We dashed back to the Deanery – still he had not turned up. Two of us dashed back again to the south lawn and there was a manhole cover twitching! He had been carried away by his photography and lost all trace of time. On our underground trips there is usually someone at the back to ensure everyone gets out.

I read a story about a mediaeval monk who became a spy in the service of the Prior. He was detected by his fellow monks and made his escape by diving down the Drain and passing round it to the far north exit, doubtless to emerge into the moat.

Esther told me of a mediaeval crypt underneath Boots the Chemists. This is a part of the cellar of a shop bought in 1183 by sub-Prior Wibart and let by him to Solomon the Mercer; the latter was a man of substance and importance in the city. The original cellar was larger and may have linked up with cellars across Mercery Lane where once stood the Chequer of the Hope a mediaeval pilgrim's hostelry.

I went down into the basement sales department of Boots and under the stairs was a small door giving access to a circular stone staircase into the crypt. It measures about 20' by 15' with a well in one corner. This is constructed of curved ashlar blocks in its lower part and brickwork above; there is an iron-barred window cut in the side of the well and the interior was lit by electricity to show a small amount of water six feet below the window. The upper part is blocked off by the basement floor. The vaulting ribs are incomplete, showing that the present cellar extended beyond its present limits.

We were also given information about a tunnel opening off a basement in Debenhams nearest the Butter market. The special interest in this tunnel was the legend that Thomas a Becket's murderers gained access to the cathedral by using this secret entry. Audrey and I met Esther in the basement – then in use as a snack bar – and met one of the shop managers. We could see the blocked-off doorway and the Management were happy to let us knock a hole in it and do our exploration provided we did it during a stock-taking weekend and had the brickwork restored by opening time on Monday morning. I even found a bricklaying architect willing to join us, to demolish and rebuild the brickwork in return for a share in the exploration.

But before the time arrived I received a letter from a former Debenham manager relating that he had actually been through that doorway, to find himself in another cellar, from which more blocked-up doorways were visible and he could explore no further.

This story of the four knights entering the cathedral precincts via an underground route could be another legend such as the tunnel rumoured to exist between Saltwood and Westenhanger castles. In Eastry near Sandwich is an extensive chalk mine system in the garden of a private house, on three different levels. It is a village story that when Becket returned from exile and landed at Sandwich, he made his way to Canterbury by using this tunnel!

Another interesting relict of Prior Wibart's time – and still in working order eight hundred years later – is the water supply he caused to be installed throughout the monastery. There is a complete system of lead piping around The Precincts; some of the old lead stand pipes are still in place and may be inspected. Wibart's water tower stands on the north side of the cathedral by the passage way between the western cloisters and the dark Entry. But the water had not been flowing for some time. Audrey and I attended a party in The Precincts given by the Vice-Dean and the doyen of the cathedral canons was present – Canon Ingram Hill. He heard I was a dowser and asked if it would be possible to find where the water system was blocked.

In the office of The Clerk of Works was a large map of the whole area and it was easy to swing my pendulum against it, using a pencil as a marker and trace the course of the pipe to its source about half a mile away. Then we went with Canon Hill to track the line of the pipe, which ran under the playground of a school in Broad Street. Nearby was a control valve on the pipe line and fired by my enthusiasm Canon Hill got in touch with Dynarod, a company that specialises in unblocking drains and a van came with one of their systems.

It was a revolving circular steel probe (turned by an electric motor) called a 'ferret' and it hauled itself up inside the water pipe for three hundred feet – without reaching the point of blockage. Dynarod then suggested they tried a jet pump which would certainly clear the blockage but might also blow a hole in the centuries-old lead pipe and send up a column of water somewhere between Broad Street and the source of the water which is a spring north-east of the city.

Canon Hill decided to risk the pipe being blown apart and Dynarod went ahead with their high pressure device. It was completely successful and water once again flowed through the ancient water system. I was able to turn a tap on the north side of the cathedral and the water flowed freely – a satisfying moment.

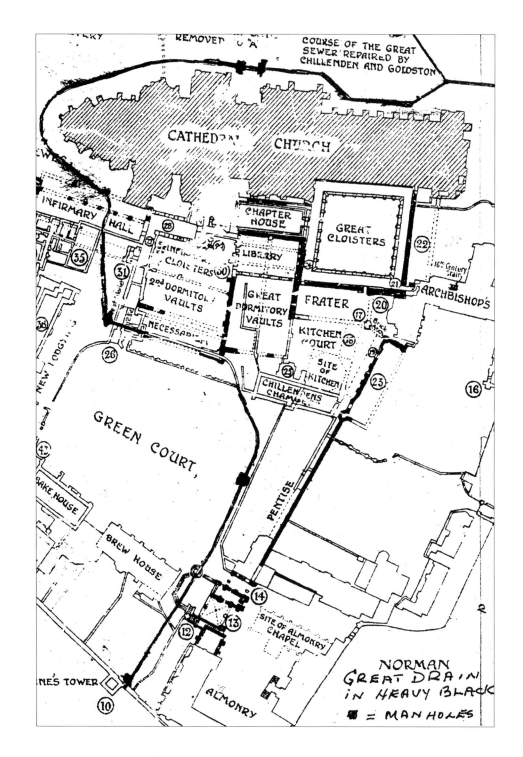

COURSE OF THE GREAT
SEWER REPAIRED BY
CHILLENDEN AND GOLDSTON

REMOVED

CATHEDRAL CHURCH

INFIRMARY HALL

CHAPTER
HOUSE

GREAT
CLOISTERS

28

LIBRARY

16ᵗʰ Century
Stairs

35

InfIRMARY
CLOISTERS

30

22

31

2ⁿᵈ DORMITORY
VAULTS

GREAT
DORMITORY
VAULTS

FRATER

21

ARCHBISHOPS

36

NECESSARY

20

17

KITCHEN
COURT

18

26

NEW LODGE

SITE
OF
KITCHEN

15

SITE OF KITCHEN

25

CHILLENDENS
CHAMBER

23

16

GREEN COURT,

43

BAKE HOUSE

PENTISE

BREW HOUSE

14

12

13

SITE OF ALMONRY
CHAPEL

NORMAN
GREAT DRAIN
IN HEAVY BLACK

NE'S TOWER

10

ALMONRY

■ = MANHOLES

The author preparing to descend into the cathedral drain; the floor lies about 8 feet below the road (halfway along west side of Green Court).

He's now under the Norman Drain (chalk blocks) 15th century brickwork further down.

Under the Deanery Garden, my wife Audrey, Dr. Esther de Waal and her son John.

Under the east end of the Cathedral

CHAPTER SIXTEEN

Snowdown Colliery

The Snowdown coal mine has closed down – there are no longer any of the four mines now working in Kent. I was lucky enough to pay a visit down the mine in December 1980 and took with me Nicholas, Nigel and our banking friend John. It was made possible by a doctor who came down the cathedral Drain with a party; he had been down the colliery and suggested I contacted the Coal Board and ask if a trip could be arranged.

Thus we found ourselves at half past seven in the morning listening to the Training Officer, Roy Harlow, as he gave us a lecture on safety down the mine – this was a constant theme all through our descent which began about eight o'clock and up again around two-thirty. We were shown how to use the 'self-rescuer' a heavy awkward sealed metal box which is opened in the event of a pit fire. Inside was a type of gas mask which converted carbon monoxide to the dioxide, there was a mouthpiece on which to bite and the nose was sealed off by a clip. I suppose the idea was that while carbon monoxide would kill you pretty quickly, the dioxide will merely suffocate you if there is no oxygen at all; at least there would be a sporting chance of making it to some exit or other before dropping flat!

We were provided with a heavy leather belt, after which Roy took us over to the lamp room where we each picked up a lamp, battery, helmet and self rescuers, attaching them to our belt. The combined weights must have totalled at least seven pounds and dragged down on our waists until our trousers were in danger of falling to our ankles. When the miners come off the shift the batteries are put on charge and left until needed again.

We were given two brass numbered tokens, one to keep with us underground and the other was handed in when we went into the shaft room. We were allowed no matches, lighters or tobacco and I was quite appalled when told that my hearing aid was a nonstarter and no camera with flash gun or electronic watch could go down the pit! The loss of my hearing aid hit me very hard indeed; I knew I would hear little of what Roy was talking about once I had taken that off. It was to do with possible methane gas, often released when the coal was cut.

This ever-present danger from 'fire damp' was responsible for many pit disasters in the past; the methane gas originated when the ancient marshy bogs and ferns slowly turned into the coal seams sixty million or more years ago, to be released again as the coal was cut. Everyone knows how the illumination problem down the pits was solved by Sir Humphrey Davy in 1816 when he invented the safety lamp. This is a paraffin lamp with the flame totally enclosed by a wire mesh gauze. The presence of fire damp causes the gas to burn with a blue flame within the gauze but the heat is conducted away fast enough to prevent the flame from spreading. Nowadays there is one lamp between eight or nine miners, merely as a fire damp check and not as an illumination which anyway is pretty feeble. The lamps are beautifully made in solid brass. All the electric equipment down the mine is specially insulated or sealed to obviate the spark risk – where even a piece of silver paper stubbing against a toecap might spark. But Snowdown, Roy said, was not a bad mine for fire damp.

The shaft we descended was three thousand feet deep, just over half a mile and my nastiest moment was standing in the cage with that sort of drop beneath me! There must have been twenty of us packed into the cages, one above the other. Not designed for comfort but for the carriage of the coal wagons, I found myself standing with one foot on a rail and the other four inches lower. The descent took just four minutes, which passed very quickly, I would have suggested two minutes..

At the bottom of the shaft was the main area with the offices and stores, fluorescent lighting, like an underground city. It was remarkable for the terrific draught coming down the shaft many times fiercer than on the London underground. Standing around was chilly and called for overalls or anoraks. Just by the shafts were the coal waggons waiting to be taken to the surface, each carrying two and a half tons of coal. It looked a lot of coal to me – until I read later that a big modern power station can consume up to ten thousand tons of coal a day! In those days most of the coal went to feed the Richborough power station near Sandwich; the quality was good and well suited for furnaces. In fact when we first bought Enbrook Manor House we found the Rayburn was fired by Snowdown coal bought direct from the pit, delivered by the Coal Board but this was stopped after two years; doubtless the local coal merchants had been protesting.

From the pit bottom we walked along to inspect one of the 'paddy engines' which drove the paddy trains – wooden trucks with facing seats in which six people are jammed so tightly opposite each other that I thought I'd be tipped out on the first corner. These paddy trains are pulled by cables hauled by the electric motors, specially built as mentioned earlier to cut the sparking risk. I guess the endless steel hawsers must be all of three miles long, passing over large pulleys at each end, while they ran over rollers placed between the rails. Roy strictly warned us not to stand or walk near the cables since, when the rails ran down into a dip (which they did pretty often), when the cable started moving again it jerked viciously upwards which would have done us a bit of no-good had we been standing astride it! Later on, walking back to the shaft bottom, I managed to trip up and fall flat on my face across the cable – which fortunately only started moving after I had picked myself up. It reminded me of the occasion in Amsterdam when I tripped over a tramline and caused a tram to screech to a halt. Maybe it was lucky I did not understand the tram driver's comments which caused hundreds of shoppers on The Roken to turn round and stare at me.

After forty minutes on the paddy train we dismounted and Roy gave us a chat with questions and answers by the side of the track. The heat was already pretty fierce in spite of the forced ventilation and after walking for a few minutes we were glad to strip off down to singlets and trousers; most of the miners wore shorts or Y-fronts. The perspiration was already streaming off me. Snowdown was the hottest Kent mine and for the first time I was gaining an idea of what coal mining was like.

No less than two hours after leaving the surface we arrived at the coal face, which was marked by the conveyor belts conveying away the coal. Up to then we had carried our mining lamps slung round our shoulders so that we could move them freely around and view our surroundings; now we had to fix them to our helmet clips. The lamp had two switches, one controlled a strongly directional beam and the other gave a weaker 'parking light'. The lead acid batteries gave up to eight hours of current and were charged between shifts in the lamp room. We now needed both hands for a bent-double crawl along a tunnel four feet high and maybe three feet wide; it was a hundred feet long. At the far end we turned left and were actually at the coal face.

This is difficult to describe, perhaps a mental drawing will help make it clear. Basically the coal face was six hundred feet long. Every two feet or so was a hydraulic jack operating a long arm forced up against the roof – four feet high. These jacks in turn were moved forward by horizontal jacks; in front of the vertical jacks was the conveyor belt – in the Nottingham coalfields the miners called it the 'Panzer'. The cut coal fell onto the belt from the trepanning machine and is carried away from the coal face to fall into the waggons we had seen further back.

The actual coal cutting device was drawn along by a chain and resembled a huge circular saw with the teeth turned inwards towards the coal face. As it turned, so water was sprayed under strong pressure over the cutting area to keep down the dust and a twenty-seven inch cut of coal fell onto the conveyor belt with each run of the trepanning machine.

The machine is then returned to its starting position, each vertical jack had its roof supports lowered and was moved forward by the horizontal jack to the new coal face, then the roof arm forced upwards against the 'rip', which was the shaley area above (and below) the coal seam. Should the coal seam not be the width of the trepanning machine then the latter also rips out stone, thereby increasing the dangers from stone dust as well as coal dust – in spite of the water.

All the water sprayed at the coal face had to be pumped out of the mine, of course. Although we thought it was surprisingly dry, Roy told us that a million gallons of water were pumped out daily into the river Stour. I might mention here that when Bettshanger colliery was first started at a depth of fifteen hundred feet it was found that the nature of the ground was such that it proved impossible to keep the railroads open, the tracks were forced up by the downward pressure so much that it was not economic to run the pit at that level and they went down another fifteen hundred feet to find more stable conditions. The original levels were still there and a gigantic lake flooded the galleries and only prevented from pouring down the shaft to the lower levels by non-stop pumping. Water is one of the great enemies of mining – only non-stop pumping enabled the Cornish tin mines to function.

We were crouched in the narrow passage way between the forests of vertical jacks and the complicated mechanical feeders, hydraulic lines etc. which ran along the passage about three feet away from the vertical jacks. As the latter all move forward, so the 'rip' is allowed to fall down so that it would seem that the hundred feet passage down which we had crawled into the actual coal face represented the former coal seam, now collapsed. The fallen shale, lying everywhere, showed clear traces of fossilised fern life when split open.

From the coal galleries we scrambled into a larger, recently made tunnel which was in process of being enlarged as a communication tunnel for the transport of machinery and wooden props. One end had been shored up; every few yards – as elsewhere in the whole mine – are arch-shaped steel girders supporting the roof but separated from the roof by split Forestry Commission logs. Nearest where we emerged from the coal face was another forest of vertical jacks supporting the roof maybe eight feet high. It was necessary to heighten the roof to accommodate the steel arches and this was demonstrated to us by an utterly terrifying process!

A leading miner attached a hawser to the nearest jack and jerked it away; it fell out and with it some of the roof props. He then pulled away two more jacks and with the removal of the last one the entire section of shale roof collapsed downward with a deafening roar, filling the whole gallery with dense dusty smoke. The roof in some way then stabilised itself for a time and the space was filled with split props and the arches put back into position.

This is a good place to explain that a major maintenance problem down the pit is the tremendous pressure exerted by the three thousand feet of strata above the galleries. The steel roof supports take the strain but transmit the thrust down, consequently the floor is forced up – it could be six feet in two months – and the rail system put out of action. Gangs have to move in to cut away the floor and relay the track; this accounted for the switchback effect we had noticed riding the paddy train. In Snowdown, Marsh Gas is not a serious problem but what can happen is that an explosion, should it happen, causes the dust in the air to ignite and travel at a thousand metres a second down the galleries. To damp down this effect there is a kind of planked ceiling leading to the coal face. On top of this is a white powdered rock – this is crushed limestone – and an explosion will shake it off the ceiling planks and control further progress of any explosive force down the gallery.

By the time we left the coal face and endured the collapse of the gallery ceiling we were extremely dirty, soaked in perspiration – the dust had settled on us as if we were flypapers, eyes with black rims round them. We gradually made our way back to the pit bottom, picking up our clothing en-route and catching another paddy train which took us a mile or so on our way. The controller of the train sat in front and he had a pole with a metal strip on the end which he used to short a pair of wires running above the track along the gallery, thereby warning the paddy engine driver he was ready to start off. We still had a half hour walk – we must have been four miles away from the main shaft bottom – by my reckoning we were underneath Bekesbourne nearing Canterbury. We had to enter and leave a number of air lock. Sometimes seven of them one after the other. The pressure of air was so terrific that Roy could only force open the doors by first sliding back a panel in each door – upon which our ears popped vigorously with the sudden change in pressure. Believe me, the ear popping experienced in jet-flying is nothing like that encountered down Snowdown colliery! We had been warned when riding down the shaft to keep swallowing to equalise the air pressure in our ears.

Once away from the shaft bottom the only illumination was that provided by our individual miners' lamps – all the work of maintenance, installing machinery – everything – had no more light than this. Although the main beam threw a considerable and powerful light, it seemed strange not to have fluorescent lamps, even ordinary floodlights down there; doubtless the risk of a spark was much too great. With this lack of light, the terrific heat – between 80° and 90°F – the dust (which seemed to remain in my eyes for days afterwards), the sheer danger of the working conditions, the necessity of being alert all the time.

Coupled with all that was the effect of working in such a hostile environment and the whole business of changing into pit clothing, descending the shaft and walking/riding to the work place maybe miles away. Then at the end of the shift the whole thing again but in reverse, never again would I contest the miners' demand for a good wage.

At the time of our visit two coal faces were being cut and each face needed eighteen miners. There were three shifts a day. The mine employed 960 men so the proportion of them actually cutting the coal was a small percentage of the work force. But the underground maintenance takes a lot of workers, then there are the surface staff – maintenance above ground, the pithead showers, the canteen, office staff. Getting out the coal was a much more complicated operation than I had ever imagined. In Kent the coal cutting is expensive because the coal seams are something like a flat plate which has been bent down saucershaped, smashed up and roughly repaired. To follow a coal seam is to find it suddenly disappear – up, down, sideways and it has to be sought out to carry it forward once more.

Roy told us that they have never had a fatal accident in Snowdown. Injuries – yes; cuts and abrasions are forever marked by scars caused by the coal dust entering the wounds, almost impossible to remove completely so it remains inside the healing tissues.

We developed a tremendous thirst down the pit through sweating so freely; a miner might drink more than half a gallon on his shift – I was glad of a swig from a proferred bottle. After we were emerged from the shaft Roy took us to the showers where we were amazed to see how dirty we were in the mirrors! Afterwards we enjoyed an excellent lunch in the canteen, sausages, chips , beans or peas and plenty of good strong tea.

It was a great disappointment that Audrey and Esther de Waal were not allowed to come with us. Parties were very small two or four was a good number to allow Roy to give the best guidance – there was often a great deal of noise – and to keep an eye on everybody in the dangerous places; I guess I was a worry, being deaf and deprived of my vital hearing aid. As far as women were concerned, there were no toilet facilities down the pit, no pithead baths for them afterwards. Another reason cited was that the sight of the miners wearing only Y fronts might disturb the more sensitive ladies – although I begged leave to doubt that! Also the amount of bad language down the pit was given as another reason although it was no more than I had been used to on the Aylesbury farm during the war, despite the land girls present and it was certainly no more than I employed myself when things did not go according to plan.

I've always felt grateful to the Coal Board for organising our visit and to Roy Harlow in particular for the absorbingly interesting trip. He was a first rate guide with a good sense of humour which failed only once after I had wandered off to retrieve my pullover, which I had left in a side tunnel. ("I wish he wouldn't do that!").

CHAPTER SEVENTEEN

Channel Tunnel

In fact there are five Channel Tunnels and the earliest three 'trial runs' still exist. the fourth one was started and finished in the 1970's – abandoned, rather – and incorporated in the final successful series of tunnels soon to become operational.

The English Channel Company was formed towards the end of 1872 and the French version three years later. Sir Edward Watkin was the dynamic chairman of the Southeastern Railway in the 1880's and he was given authority to conduct trial borings for a Channel Tunnel. He sank a shaft at Abbott's Cliff, between Folkestone and Dover and drove a heading in a north east direction for half a mile. This never went under the sea.

Sir Edward then obtained an Act of Parliament enabling him to acquire more land and he sank a second shaft at Shakespeare Cliff, to the west of Dover. He drove another heading using the same machine, which extended under the sea and was nine-tenths of a mile long.When the modern tunnels were bored this old Watkin tunnel was broken into. The machine which had drilled the tunnel was still down there in the (flooded) tunnel.

These two headings were drilled by a machine designed by Colonel F. Beaumont. It was driven by compressed air and cut a circular tunnel seven feet in diameter at a rate of thirty two inches an hour. The British Government were then getting cold feet over the drilling of a Channel tunnel which was looked at from the military aspect; distrust of the French was high and the army chief Sir Garnet Wolesley expressed strong misgivings about the whole business; finally Sir Edward was ordered to stop work. The Beaumont machine apparently broke down and as I said, was abandoned in the heading.

In 1922-3 the project was revived and a Whitaker machine was was brought to Folkestone. It had been designed during World War One to drive tunnels under the German trenches but was never put into operation. It was a substantial monster for those days since it dug a twelve foot diameter heading at nearly twelve feet per hour. It was driven by a five hundred volt electric motor consuming ninety kilowatts, supplied by a generator.

It was taken to the cliffs above the railway tunnel carrying the line from Folkestone harbour along the Warren and the generator was placed on a truck. After driving a heading of around four hundred feet it broke down and for over sixty years it could be seen sticking out of the cliffs as one went down the road to the Warren. Then towards the end of 1991 it was dug out and taken to the Eurotunnel Exhibition at Cheriton after being refurbished and put on display.

The railway line runs along the Warren; the cliffs tower above the line and the sea is far below. It is an extremely unstable area since the chalk rests on gault clay and it tends to slip seawards, especially in periods of very wet weather. During the First War the line collapsed completely. To lessen this danger the railway authorities bored out a number of headings under the railway track, extending back a hundred and ninety feet into the cliffs and these drain away surplus water. One of these headings contains the 1880 tunnel,the first one drilled by Sir Edward Watkin with the Beaumont machine.

In the summer of 1976 I organised a trip led by the late Kenneth Adams, then superintendent of British Rail in our region. He led our convoy of cars down to the huge concrete apron, built to prevent further slippage of the railway line. We walked along the sea wall under the cliffs until we reached this special heading; like all the others it was lined by old railway sleepers.

The first part of the heading was high enough to allow us to stand upright but we soon reached a low concrete archway, about four feet high, which covers the spot where Sir Edward bored his original shaft. The heading carried on again, lined with old sleepers and ended in a cul-de-sac leading off to the left. The Beaumont machine was assembled here and on the right we looked into the chalk tunnel running horizontally, heading north east at no time did it go under the sea, which surprised those of us who had not studied its history. Considering it was nearing hundred years old, the walls were in good shape – cut straight through the grey chalk with no supports whatever; the marks of the machine as it cut its way along were clearly visible. On the right wall was an inscription cut into the chalk which stated that the work was begun in 1880 by Williarn Sharp – he had to make two shots at spelling begun!

This first section had duckboards formed from old railway sleepers. Further along parts of the walls had caved-in, we had to walk on the slippery chalk. As one went in further, the walking became more difficult, the stream of water running along the floor grew deeper and finally the heading became completely flooded to the roof.

The air seemed fresh enough, no condensation marred my camera lens, yet it was oppressive down there and my face was damp with perspiration when we came out into the fresh air again.

The tunnel did not appear to be quite straight looking into the distance and our guide suggested that the Beaumont machine operators had experimented to see if the drill could be made to veer left or right as it moved forward.

In December 1983 Subterranea Britannica organised a trip down the abandoned Channel Tunnel and a party of us were taken down the sloping entrance under Shakespeare cliff in Transit vans into the tunnel itself; I believe half a mile had been bored before the Labour government called it off. The massive cutting head was still in position but the equipment behind it had gone. A few statistics are of interest. The drill had a diameter of 8.3 metres. From end to end it was 220 metres long, weighed 1350 tons and consumed 2.3 megawatts of current at 11,000 volts. It was designed to advance 6 metres per hour and handle 1300 tonnes of chalk spoil.

I heard much later that the machine had been offered for sale at £150,000 and of course I was tempted to buy it and bore a really good tunnel somewhere or other but I lacked the finance . . .

The 1880 tunnel, with John Stonestreet standing by the duckboards.
Tunnel section complete here (1975).

Walking down the tunnel started in 1975 which was aborted by the Labour Government because of cash problems! This was not incorporated with the present tunnel.

My son Nicholas examining the 1922/23 Whitworth Boring Machine.

CHAPTER EIGHTEEN

Comments on churchyards and villages

Looking back on forty years of churchyarding I am struck by four changes in the life of the countryside.

First, the state of the churchyards. When I began my career in the late summer of 1953 many village burial grounds were absolute jungles – I venture to assert that the majority of them had very little annual maintenance other than a single scything or bagging hooking. Someone might volunteer to 'have a go' at the churchyard or maybe was impressed into doing the job. None of the churchyards I was asked to look at from August until late autumn had received any attention whatsoever during the season and many of them had been jungles long before that. The grass was often chest-high, often with seeding nettles docks and thistles. In Challock there was a species of rampant yellow-flower plant which was certainly seven feet high!

When I took over my own churchyard at Newington, levelling it in the winter of 1971, the grass was shoulder high in places and no one seemed able to remember when it had last been cut – 'within living memory' was the best guess. A glance through the Church Council minute books going back to 1920 again and again contained such items as: ' The problem of the churchyard was raised again and after much discussion it was shelved until the next meeting, by when it was hoped a team of volunteers would have made a start'. Fond hopes! The volunteers never turned up or if they did, an afternoon trying to master the wilderness was enough to discourage even the hardiest worker!

The development of the motor mower had a lot to do with the improvement in the appearance of churchyards. As I said at the beginning, the average village churchyard was a wilderness and there seemed no way of tackling it unless with scythe and grass hook. And farm workers able to use a scythe skilfully were becoming a rare breed. Then I came along with my Allen Motor Scythe. This excellent machine had been in production for a number of years and was extensively used by County Council road departments to maintain roadside verges.

Doubtless in the Old Days everyone in the village was a real villager, seldom if ever leaving it, even to visit the nearest market town was an adventure. There must have been a large pool of labour available to keep the churchyard in order and do the job as a share in the church maintenance and the general upkeep of the church and its churchyard devolved upon the local people. Nowadays it seems to me that a majority of the inhabitants in a village are outsiders, living there as retired people who like the country life or those commuting into the towns around their homes. Either way such people were not likely to possess the skills necessary to wield a scythe or a grass hook.

Thus it was that when I sent out ninety copies of my circular letter asking for comments on starting a churchyard maintenance service, many of the replies came from retired army or navy men, lawyers and business executives. Because of their better education and wider experience in the world the church community was grateful to accept their help and expertise. Ex-bank managers and clerks became treasurers. Some of the farmers were churchwardens who sent in their men to tidy the churchyard but I found they were few and far between.

There was a general feeling that because one was working for the church it should be charged for at a cheaper rate than was economic! Unfortunately I shared this myself to some extent, also I never found anyone who could give me practical advice on what to charge. It was too low from the start – ten shillings an hour or fifty pence for mowing and I charged three shillings an hour for hand work plus sixpence per mile transport and some places involved a round journey of sixty miles.

Some of my letters were answered directly by the incumbent of the parish, to whom they were all addressed and I dealt directly with him; others passed on my letters to laymen to deal with. I came to realise that some parsons were more forceful than others and did not delegate the churchyard to the laity. I came to class them as 'strong' or 'weak' parsons. For example, when I was asked to level Biddenden churchyard (where I lived for three years) I was supposed to meet the Rector and a Committee of the Church Council to discuss which graves should be levelled. I duly turned up and was greeted only by the Rector and when I queried the absence of his Committee, he said 'the best committee was a Committee of one' and we would take all levelling decisions between us. Which we did and probably I started the levelling before any of the church council were aware of what was happening!

In Ickham one churchwarden was Sir Charles Empson KCMG; he and his charming wife were pillars of the church and became personal friends. The other churchwarden was a village lady who lived across the road opposite the church and never once, in all the thirty-two years I maintained the churchyard, did she ever come across and wish me the time of day! In some places I was ignored by all and sundry and in others I would expect a coffee break or a lunch on my visits, either with the incumbent or someone living nearby.

However that is life and it has been a rewarding experience travelling round the country caring for so many churchyards. I looked up the diocesan register before starting this chapter and find that I have worked in ninety-seven churchyards in Kent, four in East Sussex (Northiam and Beckley) and I surveyed a further fifteen churchyards which were not followed up. Either they were impossible to tackle with machine or else there was no money to spare or a combination of both reasons.

I recall to mind one delightful old retired colonel and his wife who became our friends and when I mowed his churchyard high on the North Downs above Wye they always invited me for lunch in their Old Rectory home. The churchyard lay on steep slope and at the top of it I was way above the level of the roof. For me to level the churchyard he had to apply for a faculty which involved advertising the plans. He did the advertising and no one objected. When he discovered the cost of :he Faculty, he decided he had had 'enough faculty', as he put it and just told me to go ahead without further ado. As a churchwarden he was a tough operator and I like to think that I follow his example. "Don't have too much truck with the Canterbury people", he often told me. Other churchwardens would never agree to anything until they made sure that their actions were covered.

The only fear I have is overdoing the Canterbury-defying business – things have grown very much tougher in recent years if errant churchwardens do not carry out their duties – there has been talk of taking really stroppy churchwardens and hanging them in gibbets at crossroads – but my fear was always being called to the cathedral, set in a hollow square of clergymen and having all my buttons snipped off while Gerald Knight or Allan Wicks played a long drone on the pedal organ . . .

An obvious change in village life is the disappearance of the parson living in his Rectory or Vicarage. There had been joint livings long before I arrived on the scene in 1953 but the process certainly gained momentum in the 1960's. More of the clergy were required to take on an additional parish; in some cases this meant his old home became surplus to current requirements and was sold to an outsider. Sometimes the cash gained in this way was used to build a new modern parsonage or else the money found its way to the diocesan funds in Canterbury. It was a running complaint in many parishes that the local church never received a penny from the sale of the sale of the parsonage – 'it all went to Canterbury'.

Many of these old parsonages could be centuries old, built in a mixture of styles including Tudor bricks and flintwork. They must have been very cold in winter without central heating and expensive in upkeep. Many of them were surrounded by anything up to two-acres of gardens. In earlier days parsons were not well paid until quite recent times and the expression 'poor as a church mouse' must have been coined to describe many of the clergy. Indeed, one of my vicars, in whose choir I sang for a number of years, was supposed to have begged the food remnants from church bazaars, teas, and other functions to feed his hungry family!

Some ancient parsonages had been replaced in Victorian times by then more modern dwellings. These were in more recent years replaced in their turn by up to date ideas. In my own parish of Newington – of Channel Tunnel fame we have an old vicarage dating back to Tudor times. Then a new Vicarage was built – a very large house – which amply accommodated one vicar's family of thirteen children. That in its turn was sold and became The Grange, turned into flats and with the advent of the Channel Tunnel the land was required by Eurotunnel and was demolished – my own son-in-law being the contractor. There has been no resident vicar in Newington for around seventy years at least.

Here are two examples. High Halden in my early days possessed a beautiful Tudor rectory. This was sold and a modern house built. Years later High Halden and Bethersden parishes were combined; the priest lived at Bethersden and the new rectory in High Halden was also sold.

Ickham rectory was a marvellous old place, centuries old, much of it in flintwork and stone. This became a casualty in 1957, the rector moved into the redundant school house (the school being closed) and the former rectory became an old peoples' home. Then the Rector retired, the new man lived just outside Whitstable and he never lived in Ickham at all. I daresay many of the old parsonages were too large, damp and chilly, costing a fortune to heat and with enormous gardens. They were willingly bought by outsiders who then spent fortunes modernising their new homes and installing central heating.

Ickham had its own rector; a mile away the other side of the Stour Wickhambreaux had its own Vicarage, the parish was combined with Stodmarsh. A mile away was Littlebourne on the A2, also with its own vicar. Now the man at Littlebourne has charge of Ickham, Wickhambreaux and Stodmarsh and the parsonages have gone in those villages.

A third example out of several I could quote. Elmstone and Preston were combined by the time I started, the vicar lived in Elmstone Vicarage. Up the road Stourmouth had its own vicar, living opposite the church down a side cul-de-sac, a long way from the village. I started in Stourmouth churchyard in 1957, the vicar soon retired and the vicarage was sold. Later the church was made redundant. Preston, Elmstone and Stourmouth are now all combined with Wingham, a very large village – so two more parsonages were lost.

I connect the decline of the parson with the falling church attendance. In the 'good old days' everyone would see their vicar or rector as he walked around his parish, visiting his flock, shopping in the village store or working in his garden. He was indeed 'their Person' with his own church and parishioners. He did not have to drive miles on a Sunday, rushing from one parish to the next and only seen rarely in those parishes beyond his own. Indeed, I have personal knowledge of clergymen who never visited any of their joint parishes during the week. "Oh, we never see our man during the week" was a remark I have heard only too often.

A thought on rising prices. In 1953 I used to buy tins of Fussels condensed milk for my coffee. It cost me a shilling [5p]. Ten years later it still cost me a shilling and then went up by an (old) penny. Nestles full cream condensed milk was a shilling and sixpence [12p]. In the spring of 1992 I paid 95p for similar tin of Nestles milk. Many of the items I bought for my lunches kept stable prices for years – potato crisps for two old pence a bag, for example. My first Atco lawn mower cost £32.00; a slightly larger Atco ten years ago was £350 or so, it is certainly a hundred pounds dearer now. My first self-propelled rotary mower cost £85; the larger models a few years later cost £185. I doubt now if there would be much change from a thousand pounds.

An important aspect of country life was the village shop. Practically all my villages possessed a general store with post office. Some villages had several shops. Appledore for example had three food shops, one with the post office, a baker and a butcher as well as a garage and blacksmith. Even a small village had a small shop which sold the essentials for day to day living.

I find it difficult to name a date when I first noticed that my sources of lunchtime food supplies were disappearing – maybe 1965? It certainly coincided with the growth of supermarkets in towns; with their greater turn-over they could easily undercut the small village store. The post office side of a business enabled it to carry on, subsidising the food department, even after trade was dwindling. Then the post office started 'rationalising' their sub post offices and that usually sounded the death knell of the whole establishment.

Another factor in the demise of the local shop is surely the greater use of the motor car. From something that only the better off inhabitants could afford to run, it became a commonplace so more people could travel into the town and buy cheaper supplies and also take their friends and relations with them. Hence also the collapse of the village bus service. The local store became merely somewhere to buy items which had been forgotten in the town shopping or to pop round for supplies when someone turned up unexpectedly.

A typical village store which we all patronised was Leonard Coombs' shop and post office in Ickham. near Canterbury. It had been founded by his great great grandfather around 1750 (I am not sure how many 'greats') and in our early days Len and his brother Frank had taken over from their parents – I can remember the father, then well in his nineties. Frank died and Len retired in 1971, handing the business over to his manager. In its heyday the brothers ran a fleet of seven vans, delivering orders over a wide area. The delicatessen department was renowned for its exotic and unusual items. So I could buy smoked oysters, bamboo shoots, ravioli and other items. The delivery service had long gone before the end of my churchyarding years in Ickham between 1953 and the end of 1984 and then Len's old manager running it told me that if the post office was closed down he would have to shut the shop the next week. The post office was closed towards the end of 1990 and Audrey and I attended the closing down sale in January 1991. Now there is no shop in Ickham and a tradition lasting for two hundred and forty years has gone.

We visited Len shortly before his ninetieth birthday and found his eye was not dim, nor his natural force abated. Besides running the shop he was the village organist – and a very good one – while Frank was in the choir. He found a lovely Snetzler organ dating from the 18th century and had it restored for the church.

Famous organists came from far and wide to play it. He had given up the post as organist but was still running his large garden unaided, except for the digging and lawn mowing.

Harking back to the old parsonages – the gardens were sometimes completely beyond the abilities of their inmates to control and while the more obvious parts round the house were – usually —tidy and cared for, the outflung areas could be as bad as any churchyard jungle. Occasionally I was asked either to do a one-off job or else cut the jungles on a regular basis, like I did for Miss Norton at Wychling. I recall one amusing visit to a vicarage outside Ashford. The incumbent was a very old man in his mid-eighties and he had asked me to call and do something about the waist-high grass and weeds in his garden. Philip and I arrived and the ancient vicar had completely forgotten all about our impending visit. However, he rallied his faculties and explained what he wanted us to do and then he went inside again, shut all the doors and windows and we never saw him again. I started work with the Allen Scythe and after a while handed it over to Philip, who seemed eager to try his hand with it, never having used it before. Aiming the machine at a large clump of nettles he proceeded to steer the Allen straight through it, realising only too late that the vicarage hosepipe was coiled up in the middle of the nettles! So the vicar ended up with ten pieces of hosepipe each a yard long instead of one length of ten yards . . .

I delayed sending in my account and then it was too late because the old chap set off on his bicycle one fine; morning, had a stroke while riding it and dropped dead on the spot. Under the circumstances I felt it kinder not to present his widow with my account.

122

Above: *Daughter Charmian with her children Lucy, Thomas and Alice (1991).*

Below Left: *Son Nicholas and Marina.* Right: *Charmian's husband Peter, with my wife Audrey, and the two girls.*

Above: *My son Nigel and* (right) *his wife .*

Below Left: *Nigel's son Timothy and* (right) *his son Mark with his grandmother,
my wife Audrey.*

CHAPTER NINETEEN

Past Thoughts and Retirement

The idea of my retirement was summed up by our church treasurer at a council meeting when she said that they expected me to go on mowing the churchyard until I was ninety; vicar Graham then chipped in to say the church would buy me a ride-on mower for my eightieth birthday . . . I can imagine that many people look forward to retiring from jobs which might have been unsatisfying and stressful, only counting off the years until they could abandon the rat race.

This never happened to me. I have always enjoyed cutting grass and working in churchyards – so peaceful, no trade unions, no boss sitting on my back, different localities every day and a feeling of something accomplished at the end of each one. Having spent thirty-two years doing an enjoyable task there seemed little point in giving it all up just because I had reached sixty-five and was perfectly active and fit. There was nothing else I wished to do and as long as my health permitted me to drive a vehicle and walk behind my mowers, there seemed no reason to bring it to an abrupt halt. As far as local lawn mowing was concerned, there were customers whose lawns I had cut for over thirty years; many were old ladies in the late eighties and I really could not bring myself to tell them I was giving them up. So I decided I would carry on with all my customers as long as they needed me. If they moved away, were put away or actually died and the home was sold, only then would I finish that job.

So gradually the lawn mowing is running down. At the start of the 1991 season there were still thirty lawns plus gardens round blocks of flats and garden work connected with the Portex factory and depots in Hythe and Folkestone. In my most active period I was maintaining forty churchyards by the end of 1984 I had reduced it to twenty-five and most of these I gave up, retaining eight favourite or nearby churchyards. The regular sixty mile round journey to Goudhurst ended after twenty-eight years and cutting out that cross country journey was a great relief. It still left the equally long journey to Northiam in Sussex to mow the parish churchyard and the little Roman Catholic churchyard round St Theresa's, founded by authoress Sheila Kaye-Smith.

This little place and Eastwell (near Ashford) were my favourite churchyards whose maintenance gave me the most satisfaction and I only gave up St Theresa's at the end of 1990 to save the cross country journeys. So at the start of my retirement season in 1985 I had eight churchyards to care for. By 1991 there were only three – Eastwell, Monks Horton and Newington, the latter being my own churchyard where I have been churchwarden for twenty years. I tried to give up Monks Horton churchyard three years ago and told the church council so when I sent in my mid-summer account. It is a small churchyard taking me only an hour to mow and in September I was walking round it before starting the mower and a voice spoke clearly within my head – as though my hearing aid had operated but in some odd way it was 'beyond' my hearing aid and actually not through my ears at all. It pleaded. "Please do not give us up!". So what could I do but tell the council I would carry on if they wanted me to? In reply, the treasurer said they had made no attempt to replace me, somehow could not believe I would be retiring after so many years. So where did the appeal come from? A corporate wish of the council or from those buried in the churchyard?

Eastwell churchyard has always been one of my best loved places. The church was allowed to decay, collapsed during 1951 and was tidied up and left as a ruin, with only the tower and a memorial chapel standing entire. The owner of Eastwell Park sowed grass in and around the nave. I was already looking after Westwell churchyard and Boughton Aluph not far away and passing between the two parishes I called in to look round Eastwell. There was a kind of air raid brick shelter built in the south corner of the ruined chancel. Peering through a narrow window, I was aghast to see two corpses lying side by side; a moment's reflection showed me they were marble effigies. Later they were removed to the Victoria and Albert Museum along with a beautiful marble statue from the mortuary chapel, known as the White Lady. They had gone by the time I took over the churchyard at the request of the Boughton Aluph churchwarden.

Eastwell church had a long and interesting history. some of which I will relate in a moment. It stands besides a forty acre lake, created from hopfields a hundred and fifty years ago. Beyond the east end of the church is a Tudor house. The church walls are built of chalk, plastered over on both sides – I believe it is a special sort of chalk termed clunch. Much of the rendering has been destroyed and therefore the chalk blocks beneath are weathering very badly. The chalk reminded me of the similar material used to construct the earliest part of the Great Drain round Canterbury cathedral, already described. The tower is built in the flintwork commonly found in Kent where little stone is available.

The most historically interesting item in the ruined chancel is a rough tombstone on the north side, constructed of concrete blocks with a concrete slabbed top – which years ago was vandalised and I had to cement it together. This marks the burial place of an illegitimate son of Richard III. The original memorial was made of Bethersden marble. He is mentioned in the church registers as being buried on December 22nd 1550.

Towards the end of the fifteenth century Sir Thomas Moyle was rebuilding his house in Eastwell Park and one day he found a bricklayer reading a book in latin. No workman would have been versed in latin nor even read English, so Sir Thomas asked this man how he came to be a scholar. He confessed that he was the natural son of the King, formerly the Duke of Gloucester and he had been brought up privately away from the court. His father had sent for him before the Battle of Bosworth in 1885, told him who he really was and told him that if he, the King, won his battle he would make his son his heir. But if he lost it to Henry Tudor then he must escape and hide, since the new king would certainly murder any possible rival claimants to his newly acquired throne.

Sir Thomas was touched by Richard's story and allowed him to build a cottage within the park where he ended his days in peace.

The original cottage was pulled down in 1689. There is a one story dwelling on the site called Plantagenet Cottage. After my article on Eastwell appeared in Kent Life in 1978 I received a letter from an old lady who had lived in the house in the early years of this century. She said it had an underground room concealed within the house, with a spring of water in one corner. However, I paid another visit not long ago and the owner told me there is now no sign of any cellar. I expect Richard Plantagenet had devised it as a hiding place, should the Tudors come seeking him.

Eastwell churchyard has a somewhat creepy atmosphere, maybe a combination of the lake and the trees surrounding the area has retained psychic memories of past events. Only once did I feel really uneasy. I had been scything rough grass and slowly became 'filled with dread'. I was becoming obsessed with the fear that a gang of men would be arriving and attack me, cutting me up with the scythe. In the end I gave in and left my work unfinished – cravenly, you may say!

On a later visit I was in conversation with a local lady to whom I confessed my fears. She told me I was not the only one to suffer distress in the churchyard and cited the case of her brother-in-law who had been walking his dog past the entrance when it stopped and refused to go any further. Looking around for a reason to account for his dog's fear, he saw some sort of a figure moving about in the churchyard.

The Tudor house beyond the churchyard was a derelict ruin in my early days at Eastwell. It was surrounded by an absolute jungle of shoulder-high nettles, docks, thistles and brambles. The first time I pushed my way through the undergrowth and entered the house, I found the atmosphere so disagreeable I came out immediately! Audrey was with me on another visit and we went over the house, crumbling into decay. A year later I was spraying weeds and a tourist hurried up to say there was a redhot wooden beam glowing in a bedroom. I sprayed water over it but telephoned the farmer on reaching home; I believe he had the fire brigade.

I met a married couple at this time who ran a pub in Cheriton. The wife related how they had visited Lake House and she had been standing in the garden and she noticed that the wilderness of weeds was parting as someone walked towards her only there was nobody there! They stood not upon the order of their going – like me in Crundale church.

In my earlier years vandalism was rife. It seemed to be a regular thing for youngsters to travel to Eastwell at the weekends and do their best to pull the place apart. The east chancel wall was reduced to almost nothing from nine feet high. Chalk blocks and big ashlar stones were flung about – some so heavy I could hardly lift them out of the way. I usually had to spend up to half an hour after my arrival just clearing the lawns of stones and rubbish. Once practically all the Kent peg tiles had been ripped of the roof of the chapel and thrown about on the grass. Set in the east wall of the tower had been three colourful ceramic tiles, the centre one depicting the Crucifixion, each about twelve inches in length. Over a period they were all attacked – it looked as if a hammer and cold steel chisel had been used. Eventually not a trace of them remained, fortunately I had taken a photograph of the group before they were obliterated. What senseless destruction . . . Destroying things of beauty for what purpose?

Eastwell will certainly be about the last of my churchyards. Often there are visitors; some cut me dead but with others I enjoy interesting conversations as they ask me about the history of Eastwell. Vandalism is much lessened; this started when the millionaire buyer of Eastwell Park had Lake House completely restored and the surrounding wilderness landscaped into gardens, had a wall built between churchyard and garden and lived in the house himself.

The park and roads leading to the church are full of partridges and pheasants. They stroll around the lane leading to the church, hardly bothering to make way for my van and staring insolently as I pass by.

CHAPTER TWENTY

Conclusion

It is now over a year since I started writing page one and the time has come to sign off. Having read it through from the beginning I realise that not all my interests have been mentioned. I have written about ghosts, divining rods and a passing reference to sleeping over running water at Enbrook Manor House, I have said nothing at all about spirit healing which for many years has been in the background of my life.

When I was eighteen I was cantering bareback on a horse when it shied at a piece of paper and threw me off, hitting my back with a hoof as it sped on. After three days I was almost unable to walk and on board a ship heading for Tangier. The Dutch masseur took me in and put me right but it remained a weak point and any heavy work on the farms could bring on an attack, which caused me to walk with a curious stooping gait for same days, with considerable pain.

I suffered from backache pains and twinges for many years; levelling churchyards humping curbstones about hardly helped. Then I heard of a spirit healer in Yorkshire, Fred Partington and I wrote to him after a specially severe attack of back pain (it was muscular, I must explain, not caused by misalignment of the spine). The day after he received my letter I got out of bed and suddenly realised my back pains had vanished, I was walking normally again. I wrote to him the evening after I had lost the top finger joint under a slate grave slab and as I said earlier, there was never any pain after the local anaesthetic had worn off – even although my finger felt 'on fire' with the pain, it simply failed to register in my mind as 'pain' but rather as a 'memory of pain in the past' being the best description.. it was quite uncanny! And the healing prevented Beetle Dog from gnawing away his paw after his accident and before his death from Leukaemia.

I did not wish to bother Fred Partington unduly and after another bad bout of backache I finally appealed to 'whoever was helping me to do something about it' next morning I was walking normally again, pain vanquished.

Just before we moved to Enbrook Manor House in Cheriton I slipped on a step and hit the back of my neck. A month later I could hardly turn my head, my neck was becoming very painful. I wrote to my healer explaining the situation and the next night I was woken up at 2.45 in the morning, completely paralysed and then ' someone' caught hold of my head and my shoulders and gave a powerful twist; there was a terrific CLICK!! within my cervical vertebrae and then I found myself able to move hand and foot again. I was so astonished that I woke up Audrey and told her what had just happened. The following night I woke up again at the same time, paralysed again and then strong fingers massaged my neck for some minutes. Then that stopped and I was able to move again.

Since then my neck has been little trouble after the sleeping over running water business and my Middlesex Hospital check-up which included a neck X-ray, nothing amiss was found. So that convinced me – if further proof were needed – of the reality of spirit healing. Not just vague sensations but real strong arm stuff delivered in the middle of the night. Some spirit doctor had got to grips with my body and used a lot of force to put my vertebrae back into alignment.. Also the response to my appeal to have my back pain cured showed that I could contact the healing process directly – and if it worked for me then maybe other people could be helped.

On two occasions I have woken up in the darkness and clearly seen two spirit forms in the room when I was having healing. I don't know if they gave off their own illumination or if it was my spiritual vision which enabled me to see them.

I was given another comforting experience when I woke up early one morning and found myself floating several feet above the bed and I was thinking how extraordinary it was to realise I was asleep in bed at the same time I was awake floating above myself and to realise I was thinking with a mind that to all intents and purposes was quite invisible. Then my astral body slowly sank down and entered my physical body; I had the sensation of fitting into it and wriggling into my fingers and toes as if putting on gloves. So I know from personal experience that I can exist outside my physical body and retain my own personality. This lessens the fear of death, naturally, just a change from lower vibrations to a higher form. But also like leaving a country and all one's friends and life behind.

Just one more experience and I shall be finished ("And thank God for that!") I hear someone mutter. You will remember the old family friend who conducted the seance in Appledore church. She died many years later and one night I was praying for her and thought – silly to think she needs my prayers, she is an expert, having been mediumistic during her life-time. I was suddenly pushed over, causing me great astonishment and a rapid retreat from my prayers. Some years later I had occasion to consult a medium about whether we should sell Enbrook Manor House. I bought a copy of Psychic News and selected a medium from the advertisements, she lived in Devonshire.

In a long reply, she started by saying that three people had appeared to her, each carrying a red rose – their symbol of affection for me. Two were in old-fashioned costume but the third was an old lady in modern dress who had not been dead for long. She was very cheerful and laughed as she said: "I made Michael jump!". So I knew at once who the lady was and that to me was a convincing proof that we do indeed survive death and exist elsewhere.

CHAPTER TWENTY-ONE

Deafness

A local friend read my finished typescript and said he wanted to know much more about deafness. He was aware I have been deaf all my life and he reckoned I was in a good position to offer words of advice, comfort and admonition.

He pointed out that Beethoven composed some of his greatest music after he had become totally deaf and what did I think of that? Easy to answer. Beethoven during his earlier hearing years had gained intimate knowledge of the piano and orchestral sounds, both individually and collectively. The fact that he became stone deaf did not detract from his musical memories and he heard the music he composed in his inner ear and would have known exactly how it sounded. I do not see why it has to be hailed as one of the wonders of the world. Apparently Mozart heard entire musical works within his mind and all he had to do was to write them down; the composing had already been done for him. But then he was a musical genius. I have always found it quite astonishing how he listened to some music in the Sistine Chapel which lasted over an hour and he went home and wrote down the whole service from memory, the music had been a carefully guarded secret until then.

I, on the other hand, have never heard music sounding as it appears to all you normal hearing readers. My upper range ends about two octaves above middle C and with my hearing aid it extends a few notes higher; thereafter it is just a series of taps, the hammers striking the strings. The quality of a note depends very much on the high pitched transient tones – which cause one piano to sound different from another or one violin from another. I have absolutely no way of telling the quality of an instrument and so to some extent I cannot distinguish between one orchestral instrument from another, beyond obvious depth of tone – as a double bass or a bassoon.

So I cannot imagine anyone in my position being able to compose music – orchestral music, any more than a colour blind person could paint a picture of the scene in front of him in glowing colours. He surely must be confined to drawings in black and white and shades of grey. He could certainly create magnificent drawings but their quality surely depends on the composition and skill displayed in the picture. So I don't see how a deaf from birth person could create, say a piano concerto, without the musical memory needed for such a feat. This is not to say I have never written simple tunes for the piano. My earliest four line melody was written when I was thirteen and in love with Nancy Ronan, the Irish nurse who looked after me when I had my appendix removed. How sweet and painful is one's first love!

Well, I hear you say, put on a hearing aid and the problem is solved! It is not, because aids have their limitations. Yes, if I turn up my volume and strike a note on the piano I shall hear more than my unaided ears will give me but make a chord and the same volume position will be far too loud.

Consider a listener in a concert hall in front of a full orchestra of eighty players. A quiet passage is being played but our normal listener can follow the strands of the music with perfect clarity. The orchestra starts a crescendo; finally all the musicians are hard at it full blast, the conductor on his rostrum lashing himself into a frenzy. Yet the listening ear is well able to accommodate itself to the huge increase in decibels. There is no need to wince or put hands over ears.

If I am that listener, in order to hear the quieter passages, I have to turn up the volume control and then, as the orchestra warms to its task, progressively turn down the volume because the level of sound is becoming painful. I believe some hearing aids contain a limiting device which will by-pass the excessive volume and prevent overloading but my aid does not do this. I have a small tape recorder which has this over-load system which means I can set it at a good level to pick up quiet sounds and it will cut down on the decibel level when it is liable to distort the recording. Very useful . . . but the recording will not be a true one, since the music is compressed into a narrower range.

What about low notes? I hear these very well indeed and therefore simply love low tones! Canterbury cathedral organ used to have a superb open metal thirty-two foot pedal stop, just below the threshold of normal hearing. It used to creep along the floor of the choir and shake my trouser legs – the pipes themselves being (like the rest of the organ pipes) around fifty feet up in the south triforium. When Noel Mander re-built the organ (and reduced it from four manuals to three), he removed this splendid open metal stop; it lay horizontally and took up a lot of space for what was really very little effect. I understood Mr. Mander's decision but have not forgiven him this bit of vandalism.

Obviously the lack of higher notes in my range coupled with a greater sensitivity to low notes makes the whole concept unbalanced. The hearing aid brings in the higher registers but it is fairly useless with the low tones; I rely on my own hearing for that.

After a year as Appledore organist I acquired my Medresco hearing aid and tried it during a practising session at the organ. The quality of the sound was so entirely altered I simply could not face the transition! I did try it for one service but found coping with the different levels of sound needed for gaining my cues and then playing the organ too much of a bother and I gave up, muddling along as before. I occasionally deputise in my own church of St Nicholas Newington (site of the Channel Tunnel) where the organ is at the back of the church and to pick up my cues from the other end I have to raise the level of hearing, only to reduce it before starting to play or the noise level is excessively painful. I would be pleased if anyone can suggest a way out of this problem.

Every year for the past twenty-one years I have attended the Archdeacon's Visitation service in Canterbury cathedral for the newly elected churchwardens and sides persons. Until recently listening has been an ordeal. Certainly there is an extensive microphone and loudspeaker system. Even normal hearing people have difficulty following what is said because of the cumulative effect of the echoes. The archdeacon is away up on the chancel steps, quite beyond lip-reading range from where I like to sit and I never understood a single word – unless I had the words in front of me, the service sheet or copy of the Visitation sermon. My aid picked up not only the echoes but also all the sounds inherent among a large assembly of people – hisses, groans, stomach rumbles, muttered snatches of conversation, sneezes, coughs, nose blowing . . . During the service the archdeacon asks the churchwardens to rise to their feet and repeat the Oath after him or his legal deputy. I never had the least idea what it was all about and rather than stand on my feet with my mouth shut, I used to recite a jingle of rubbish usually starting: "Criggly crog nunkeley, isbar worthan beerleber rumwolding issbar . . ."

But with the loop system being laid around the choir all this nonsense disappeared. By switching my aid from microphone to loop, every sound in the cathedral vanished (without the microphone I was hardly aware of the echoes) and speaking clearly within my head, like the voice of Almighty God, I heard every syllable uttered by Michael Till. It was absolutely magical! Only one disadvantage – on loop the sound of the organ and singing was mostly blocked off which made it difficult to sing with enjoyment. But I had another string to my bow – an additional switch position which combined microphone and loop inputs which gave me the ability to cut down on the echoes yet still be able to join in the singing.

These large resonant buildings make it very difficult for the deaf. I remember the cathedral chapter house where Audrey and I attended a conference on Church Maintenance. Knowing the chapter house to be completely impossible to listen in, I wrote previously to the organiser asking if a loop system could possibly be installed – and it was being tested as we went in. Its organiser asked me to listen while he worked out the volume setting; it was the first time I had encountered a loop system and again, as later in the cathedral choir, the effect was wonderful. Complete silence except for the speaker's voice. One gentleman placed the microphone on the floor yet from there it still picked up and relayed to my ear the lecturer.

Many theatres now have a loop system installed and while it can be a great help in enabling me to follow the script, I still have difficulty in understanding although the sound is loud enough within my ear, I cannot distinguish the words, could be any language. This is the fault of my hearing, not of the system.

This leads to another aspect of listening – the ability to understand speech without lip reading (as a loudspeaker). I have never been one of the deaf with good lip-reading ability. For me it is somewhat hit and miss – so many words with similar lip movements, BEAR and BARE, for example. My mind acts like a computer, faster than I can think, assessing every word not entirely understood, comparing the sound with the lip movements. If the speaker is not very clear and/or I am not very close, the listening and assessment becomes very tiring and my attention will begin to flag. The loop is better than direct microphone but there are times when a speaker will not use it, convinced his voice is so clear he has no need of the loop! This is quite wrong; I assert that the loop system is better than direct microphone.

Readers will remember how friends used to write down the words of songs for me, as The Way You Look To-night, because I have never been able to follow songs unless I had the words in front of me. Even such beautiful singers like Count John Macormack singing "Schubert's Serenade or Richard Crookes Dearest the day is over/Endeth the dream divine were complete gibberish to me until someone had written down the words. This defect in my hearing was often the cause of my downfall in Appledore church when I lost my place in the service book, following both words and music together. I had to scour the text frantically trying to gain a clue where we had got to, to catch a word I saw in front of me so that I could follow again. Sometimes it was the final end of a prayer which I heard (if I was lucky) 'through Jesus Christ our Lord' and I could play the amen.

No one who had never had to suffer this mishap can understand the amount of misery this disability caused me, week after week for seven years. If I managed a service without at least one mistake, that was a matter for congratulation.

I could have put a stop to this nonsense by informing the clergy how hard it was for me to follow the prayers and come in with the amens. It would have been easy to dictate that from henceforth all amens would be said – that would mean the prayers would have to be said, of course. In Appledore the responses, Creed, Lord's Prayer and Collects were all intoned on G. My organist's musical copy contained a series of modulations beginning in the key of G, moving into C and then into all sorts of assorted keys, finally returning to G (or C) for the amen. As I had as much knowledge of modulating as a persian cat, and often becoming bored with the printed versions, I used to follow my own ideas, sometimes becoming lost in an impossibly remote key, thereby obliging me to return with a horrible jerk to G (or C) for the amen! No one ever commented on my musical antics and if there had been a criticism I would have said: All right, Buster! Go and do it yourself .

Back to hearing aids again. My aid is indispensable and I would be lost without it and increasing years see my hearing loss growing. The aid fails me in public places such as pubs, parties, coffee in the chapter house – anywhere a group of people are chatting together. The microphone gathers up all the sound from around me and directs it into one ear – so-called directional microphones don't seem to make much difference. It is a diabolical cacophony and sorting out what one's speaker is saying is almost impossible; probably better to remove the aid and have your friend speaker louder. Even the old fashioned hand cupping behind an ear is quite effective.

I have two identical aids and have tried wearing both together but do not like it. Two volume controls to manage, two ears battered instead of only one. The other area where aids come to grief is in private conversations between groups of people. There can be a huge disparity in the quality and loudness of the speakers. Audrey's voice is very clear and gives me no trouble but another voice can have a soft bleating quality causing my volume input severe problems. One is too loud and the other too soft. Discussion groups were my especial bugbear, a group of us round a table discussing a topic. I always had the greatest difficulty following the trends of thought; the nervous strain finally made me refuse to take part in any further discussion groups or 'workshops'.

I try to avoid chatting in places with hard wall and floor surfaces, the echoes are dreadful. In my gardening work I keep my aid on, with the volume turned down to cut out background and traffic noise. People often stop and talk to me or call me from afar with a greeting – or offer of a cup of tea – and my normal hearing means I am cut-off from my surroundings. Besides, if the aid is turned off, that ear is pretty well out of action and the other ear is not so good.

I meet a number of old people who have been provided with hearing aids, tried them and put them away rather than endure the business of learning to use them. I have an old lady friend of over ninety. The NHS provided her with an aid and she never wore it because she could not fit the solid ear mold into her ear! Her fingers had not the manual dexterity to insert it so consequently she had had it for three years without using it. I suppose the NHS service, five miles away, had never checked to see if she was happy with the service.

I do not like the solid ear moulds and prefer those with a thin loop which slips into the ear lobe, easier to grasp and insert and also lighter. My hearing aid man came over and made her a mould similar to mine, which she was able to slip in more easily. But she would not wear it consistently. I told her that inserting the aid only when she needed it was not a good plan; she should wear it all the time and turn it off when there was no call for its use. Recently she asked me to put in a new battery, which I did but it still did not work. After cleaning the contacts it did not work, finally I realised that the volume control was turned right down. She put the aid back in again and I turned the control until an expression of delight came over her face – she could hear again!

The fact is that she had been wearing the aid for some months with the new ear mould yet she had no idea there was a volume control. I guess my consultant had first put it in for her and adjusted the volume for her needs but he had assumed she knew about the control of sound. Surely the original NHS department had instructed her in its use? It seems not.

Other thoughts on hearing aids? I never wear mine in hot weather when I am working outside. The salty sweat from my ear and hair is death to the sensitive electronic system if it gets inside the microphone or battery compartment. I ruined two aids before I cottoned on to this. The discolouration within the battery compartment can be astonishing and the contacts need scraping to clean them. In wet weather either I take off the aid or wear a hat.

As I told my old friend, I recommend wearing the aid all the time and if not in immediate need of its use I turn it off – and do this by opening slightly the battery compartment. I never use the switch to turn it off as this increases wear on the four positions of microphone, microphone/loop, loop and off. They are close together and according to my hearing aid consultant Douglas, best used as little as possible.

The earpieces have varied, some are more comfortable than others. Obtaining a good fit is a knack not always acquired by the supplier and I have had moulds which made my ear quite sore, but overcame this by using a piece of glasspaper to rub down the high spot causing the soreness. It has to be a reasonable fit to avoid acoustic feed back which becomes more of a problem as the volume is increased. The whistling produced can be an embarrassment! I recall an organist friend who told me he had heard a pipe on the organ sounding during a lesson and he pushed in the stops one by one to eliminate the offending pipe without any effect and he then realised the whistling was coming from a hearing aid in the congregation!

I read an account about the impossibility of explaining colour to a blind-from-birth person. What colour is milk? It is white. What is white? The colour of snow, of writing paper . . . You cannot explain what colour looks like (although I believe it feels different to a sensitive blind person).

In a similar way friends ask me what I think of a bird singing, do I enjoy listening to blackbirds? But I have never heard bird song and really have no idea what it sounds like. We can be in a wood on a silent day and Audrey tells me to try and hear the singing around us. I turn up my hearing aid but cannot ever hear anything; it is far too high for me. With aid volume in normal position I hear the cuckoo, doves or a woodpecker drilling into the tree. I find doves and cuckoos very boring after a few minutes but at least I can shut them off.

One bird I wanted to hear was the owl which lived in the trees round our old home. One very still night Audrey said 'our owl' was hooting again and I went into the garden, turned up my aid and was rewarded by hearing this lovely quavery hooting call. You hearing people can have little conception of the tremendous thrill caused by finally hearing an owl hooting when in my mid-fifties. I have no idea what the Dawn Chorus sounds like; maybe tapes are available of bird song, did not the BBC have a famous recording of a nightingale singing in some wood? Perhaps with earphones and volume turned well up I might finally gain some idea of what birdsong sounds like.

Fortunately tinnitus does not trouble me to any great extent. Generally it is just a faint buzzing, only obvious if I stop to listen and a severe cold produces a sustained humming usually on middle D – I tested notes on the piano until middle D tuned in with my hum. The alarming sounds reported from real sufferers seem to make life very difficult; one friend says she has a clock ticking away must of the time. Occasionally I have a loud PIIIINNGG! sounding for a few seconds but it does not keep repeating itself.

As they say, what you have never experienced you never miss. Very true, I dare say. But there are moments of depression when one needs to hear so badly, to listen to music as it really sounds. perhaps when I arrive on the Other Side I shall begin to realise what has been missing from my life. Not that I am complaining, there must be a reason for my deafness as expounded in the final chapter of my earlier book. There are compensations. What? Well, at the moment I cannot think of any – yes – when I was seven and went to my Harley Street ear nose throat consultant, he told my mother that if there was ever another war she would be thankful her son was deaf and this came true thirteen years later when I gave up the Middlesex hospital and was turned down by the recruiting authority.

I recall endless moments of unhappiness caused by poor hearing, especially in my teenage days dancing with pretty partners and being unable to understand much of their chatter, failing to attract them. I imagined them telling their friends in contemptuous fashion: Oh, he's deaf, failing to recognise my humour and hidden depths. That was all of sixty years ago now and I am older and hopefully wiser.